A MILLION LITTLE MIRACLES
STUDY GUIDE

REDISCOVER THE GOD WHO IS
BIGGER THAN BIG, CLOSER THAN CLOSE,
AND GOODER THAN GOOD

A Million Little Miracles

STUDY GUIDE

MARK BATTERSON

MULTNOMAH

A Multnomah Trade Paperback Original

Published in the United States by Multnomah, an imprint of Random House, a division of Penguin Random House LLC.

MULTNOMAH is a registered trademark and the M colophon is a trademark of Penguin Random House LLC.

Author is represented by the literary agency of The Fedd Agency, Inc., P.O. Box 341973, Austin, Texas 78734.

Some material is adapted from *A Million Little Miracles* by Mark Batterson, copyright © 2024 by Mark Batterson, first published in the United States by Multnomah, an imprint of Random House, a division of Penguin Random House LLC, in 2024.

Trade Paperback ISBN 978-0-593-19287-0
Ebook ISBN 978-0-593-19288-7

The Cataloging-in-Publication Data is on file with the Library of Congress.

Printed in the United States of America on acid-free paper

waterbrookmultnomah.com

2 4 6 8 9 7 5 3 1

Most Multnomah books are available at special quantity discounts for bulk purchase for premiums, fundraising, and corporate and educational needs by organizations, churches, and businesses. Special books or book excerpts also can be created to fit specific needs. For details, contact specialmarketscms@penguinrandomhouse.com.

CONTENTS

A NOTE FROM MARK

Have you ever experienced a miracle? Witnessed one? Been part of one?

I know many people who would answer "No." But with all due respect, you have never *not*. We are surrounded by a million little miracles! In fact, let me push that envelope—you are one! Yes, *you*. Of course, that isn't a testament to you. It's a testament to the God who made you.

You are fearfully and wonderfully made. Your body is an intricate ecosystem with trillions of cells. The organs and systems that work in harmony with one another are nothing short of miraculous. And the same can be said of your brain. The most powerful supercomputer on the planet can't do what your brain does! You are a miracle. Don't let anyone tell you otherwise!

More than eight billion people live on planet Earth, but not one of them has your fingerprint. The same is true of your eyeprint and sweatprint. And when it comes to your voiceprint, no other voice exactly matches your audio frequency!

Why did God make us this way? To remind us that each of us is invaluable and irreplaceable—a walking, talking miracle.

Remember the old axiom: *Fact is stranger than fiction*? It's true. We live on a planet that is spinning at 1,000 miles per hour while speeding through space at 67,000 miles per hour.[1] How do we not get dizzy? Or fall off? We are glued by gravity—and, I might note, just the right amount. If gravity were any stronger or weaker, it would radically alter reality as we know it. Everything from blood circulation to ocean tides is a function of gravity, as is your vertical leap.

When was the last time you praised God for gravity? I'm guessing *never*, but I hope that changes during this study. The truth? We owe the Creator a heartfelt thanks for all four fundamental forces—gravity, electromagnetism, strong nuclear force, and weak nuclear force. Nearly everything we enjoy is a result of these fantastic four. It's how we watch television. It's why we can stick a magnet to a fridge. It's how planets stay in orbit.

Simply put, "a million little miracles" is an understatement. There are also a billion big miracles. And lots of miracles in between.

But back to my original question: Have you ever experienced a miracle? Throughout this study, I hope you come to the realization that you've never gone a day *without* a miracle. And you never will. That's worth celebrating! Instead of taking them for granted, take them for gratitude! Why is this so important? Because whatever you don't turn into praise turns into pride.

We're going to dig deeper into these realities in the pages of this study. We're going to explore these *everyday miracles*, pinpoint the proper Source of those miracles, and identify the right response.

Are you ready to wrap your mind around a million little miracles? Let's go!

—*Mark Batterson*

HOW TO USE THIS GUIDE

tart each session in this study guide by reading the corresponding chapter in the book *A Million Little Miracles*. (Read chapter 1 of the book before engaging session 1 of the study guide, chapter 2 before engaging session 2.) As you read, remember to allow yourself—and God—whatever space is necessary to work in your heart and mind.

As you work through each session of the study guide, you'll find four sections designed to help you absorb and apply the major themes of the book:

- **Start with a Miracle:** Each session will begin with a quick meditation on something miraculous in our world—something that points us toward the reality of our Creator and the way He works in our lives. This section will also give you a chance to think about your own experiences with these kinds of miracles.
- **Study the Words:** Next, you'll spend some time digging deeper into the primary themes covered in the chapter. This material will reinforce what you've read, including callouts of key passages. It will also provide an opportunity for you to record your own thoughts and answer key questions connected with those passages.
- **Study God's Word:** Now it's time to focus specifically on Scripture. You'll read a short passage that expands or illustrates the main theme of the session, and you'll work

through questions designed to help you unpack the text and connect it with your life.

- **Carpe Wonder:** *Carpe diem* means "seize the day," and it's a great way to live. But let's up the ante and *carpe wonder.* In this final section, you'll find opportunities to implement important principles from the session. You'll identify specific ways to apply those principles to your everyday rhythms and routines.

All the material in each session works well for both personal study and group interactions. That said, miracles love company! I encourage you to gather with a group of people to unpack each session. If you do, be sure to use the prompts and questions included in the Leader's Guide at the back of this resource.

A MILLION LITTLE MIRACLES
STUDY GUIDE

COUNT THE STARS

Based on chapter 1 of *A Million Little Miracles*.

START WITH A MIRACLE

Did you know scientists have snapped pictures of black holes in intergalactic space? Not just one either. They've photographed multiple black holes—including Sagittarius A. It's a supermassive black hole at the center of the Milky Way. Though the pictures themselves may not be as impressive as the ones taken by the James Webb Space Telescope—the black holes look like colorful donuts—the fact that they've been photographed at all is a monumental feat. They are black holes, after all!

Black holes exist thousands, tens of thousands, even millions of light-years away from Earth. Some are small enough to fit in your pocket, yet stellar black holes can be twenty times as large as the sun. And some supermassive black holes have a mass that is millions to billions times the mass of the sun. They are so dense that nothing can escape their gravitational pull—not even light.

Think about that last point for a moment. When we look at a photograph of a black hole, we are seeing what is unseeable. We've captured something that captures light itself. We have the privilege of studying a phenomenon that is unfathomable and in many ways unimaginable.

What are the chances that humans—such small beings with such obvious limitations—would have the opportunity to interact, even in this tiniest way, with such cosmically significant wonders? Is that not miraculous?

When have you been awestruck by something from the natural world? Do your best to draw that moment in the space below.

How have your interactions with nature informed or transformed your relationship with God?

_____

_____

_____

_____

STUDY THE WORDS

One of the tragedies of what we call modern life is that it's become a lot more modern and a lot less life. Modern conveniences have separated us in very real ways from the actual experiences that make up our lives. And as amazing as it is, so has technology.

Screens are Exhibit A. How much of our time is spent looking at life through a screen rather than experiencing life through our own senses? Actually, how much of our lives are spent looking at screens to vicariously watch *other people* enjoy meaningful experiences? Too much.

When we lose touch with nature, we lose touch with the God of nature. More specifically, one of the ways we're impaired by our current comforts and conveniences is that we've insulated ourselves from the natural world.

> I appreciate the roof over my head. I appreciate air-conditioning, running water, indoor plumbing, high-speed internet, and hundreds of other luxuries that technology affords us. I prefer glamping to camping. I once hiked the Inca Trail to Machu Picchu, but I brought along an inflatable mattress. Did I feel less manly than the other guys in our group? Yes, I did. Did I regret it? Not for a single second of sleep!
>
> I'm grateful for the comfort and convenience of modern life, but there is a hidden tax. When we lose touch with nature, we lose touch with nature's God. Edison's lightbulb is a gift to early birds and night owls, but it fundamentally altered the built-in rhythms of sunrise and sunset. Refrigeration allows us to enjoy exotic foods from faraway places, but farm-to-table is lost in the mix. If we aren't careful, we'll fall victim to the numbing effect that Robert Michael Pyle called the "extinction of experience."[1] We'll stop climbing trees. We'll become mere spectators to life. We'll settle for creature comforts.
>
> —MARK BATTERSON, *A Million Little Miracles*

How has this "extinction of experience" impacted your life in recent years?

It's difficult to draw the line between being comfortable and being too comfortable—but that's a line we must identify if we want to enjoy the former without drifting into the latter. What are some of the luxuries or technologies that bring comfort and convenience to your life? Are there any that bring too much comfort and convenience?

Emotions are a critical part of the experience of life. Often it's our emotions that tell us when we are truly *living* rather than merely existing. One of the core emotions—and evidence that we are living life the way it was meant to be lived—is *wonder*. Or we might call it reverence. Or amazement. Or good old-fashioned awe.

Nature inspires wonder in us. There's something about standing at the top of a mountain or feeling the force of a crashing wave that reminds us just how big the world is—and just how small we are. That's because the natural world offers a direct pipeline to the Creator of that world.

But nature isn't the only element of life that's awe-inspiring. Remember your first kiss? Or the first time you held your child in your arms? Or the first time you heard what became your favorite song?

> Where do we find awe? The answer is, *anywhere!* I love art galleries and national parks, but that may not be your jam. Awe is more of a mindset than a circumstance. It might have more to do with pace than place. The psalmist said, "Be still, and know that I am God."[2] Notice the change of pace prescribed by the psalmist. The slower you go, the more you notice! There is something about awe, no matter when or where we experience it, that deactivates the default mode network in the brain.[3] This is how heaven invades earth.
>
> —MARK BATTERSON, *A Million Little Miracles*

When was the last time you were in awe of something—the last time something affected you so profoundly that you got goosebumps?

_____

_____

_____

Review the concept of a two-foot field trip on page 10–11 of A Million Little Miracles. *What might that look like today? What are the "tents" that obscure our view of God?*

_____

_____

_____

Do you want to experience more miracles? Or, more accurately, do you want to become more aware of the miracles that are happening all around you? One way to do that is to make an intentional effort to get out of your normal routines. Routines are incredibly important, but when routine becomes routine, it's time to change the routine.

Remember the formula from chapter 1?

Change of pace + change of place = change of perspective

Routines and miracles mix like oil and water. Meaning, they don't. If you're unaware of everyday miracles, there's a good chance your life has become too routine. Consider taking a step back. Mix things up. Do something you've never done so that you can experience something you've never felt.

I get some of my best ideas when I'm hiking or biking or running. Why is that? Scientific studies suggest that exercise intensifies brain-wave amplitude and frequency. It also improves slow-wave sleep, which reduces brain fog.[4] Even something as simple as a change in posture can shift your perspective. When I kneel, that body posture affects my heart posture. I also close my eyes to open them! . . .

If you want to experience miracles, sometimes it's as simple as introducing a change of pace or a change of place. Go on a silent retreat. Establish a Sabbath ritual. Do a social media fast. Pick up a copy of *Draw the Circle*, and take the forty-day prayer challenge.[5] You do you, but do it differently than you've done it.

—MARK BATTERSON, *A Million Little Miracles*

What are some of the routines that define your typical week? How do those routines benefit you?

_____

_____

_____

_____

What steps could you take this week to change those routines and intentionally experience something new?

_____

_____

_____

_____

STUDY GOD'S WORD

Many people in Scripture encountered God in goosebump-inspiring fashion. Adam and Eve walked with God in the cool of the day. Abraham was part of a covenant ceremony complete with fiery torches and God's presence. Ezekiel saw visions of God filled with thunder and lightning and strange creatures and a spinning throne.

But Moses's unexpected encounter with God may have been the coolest:

One day Moses was tending the flock of his father-in-law, Jethro, the priest of Midian. He led the flock far into the wilderness and came to Sinai, the mountain of God. There the angel of the LORD appeared to him in a blazing fire from the middle of a bush. Moses stared in amazement. Though the bush was engulfed in flames, it didn't burn up. "This is amazing," Moses said to himself. "Why isn't that bush burning up? I must go see it."

When the LORD saw Moses coming to take a closer look, God called to him from the middle of the bush, "Moses! Moses!"

"Here I am!" Moses replied.

"Do not come any closer," the LORD warned. "Take off your sandals, for you are standing on holy ground. I am the God of your father—the God of Abraham, the God of Isaac, and the God of Jacob." When Moses heard this, he covered his face because he was afraid to look at God.

— EXODUS 3:1–6

Take a moment to circle the specific emotions Moses experienced in the passage above. How are those emotions connected with the practice of worship?

———————————————————————————————

———————————————————————————————

———————————————————————————————

———————————————————————————————

Verse 4 says, "When the LORD saw Moses coming to take a closer look, God called to him." What did Moses need to turn away from to take a closer look at what God was doing?

———————————————————————————————

It's no coincidence that this divine appointment happens when Moses was "far into the wilderness." God could have spoken to Moses while sitting in his favorite chair or as he ate breakfast at home. That would have been more convenient for Moses, right? More comfortable?

But God waited until Moses left the comfortable confines of his routine. He set up a fireworks show that was sure to attract Moses's attention—but He didn't speak until Moses responded. Only when the shepherd turned aside from the flock did God call out to him.

Notice what God said: "Moses! Moses!" This was a personal experience. The Creator of the universe was working through His creation to send a specific message to a specific person. When Moses responded to what God was doing in the world, God called him by name. More than that, He spoke with Moses about the mission and purpose of his life: "Now go, for I am sending you to Pharaoh. You must lead my people Israel out of Egypt" (verse 10).

What are some factors (people, problems, routines, distractions) that hinder your ability to perceive God or connect with Him? Be specific.

What have you learned from God about the mission and purpose of your life? Can you put that calling into a sentence or two?

_____

_____

_____

_____

CARPE WONDER

The world is filled with miracles. Day in and day out, God interacts with us in ways that are both immeasurably wonderful and incredibly precise. He speaks with us. He gives guidance. He protects. He corrects. He loves us enough to love us in every way possible.

In other words, God is present. He's *omnipresent.* All that's absent is our awareness.

One of the sad realities of modern life is that we've become too busy to notice these little miracles, these holy moments. That's the bad news.

The good news? All we have to do is open our eyes to the obvious! We must take time to notice. Make that your mission over the course of this study! Keep an eye out each day for the kinds of miracles highlighted in the book and in this study guide. As you notice those miracles, write them down. If it helps, record them in a miracle journal.

Let's start with today.

MY MIRACLES: *During this past week, how has God arrested your attention through His creation? And that includes people! Write down any examples that come to mind.*

_____

_____

_____

_____

What steps will you take this week to be more aware of little miracles in your life?

_____

_____

_____

_____

REMINDER: Read chapter 2 of *A Million Little Miracles* before engaging session 2 of this study guide.

PLAYFELLOWS

Based on chapter 2 of *A Million Little Miracles*.

START WITH A MIRACLE

Can you guess the largest life form that has ever lived on our planet? No, it's not a dinosaur. It's not a woolly mammoth. It's not even some tricky answer like a swarm of locusts or interconnected fungi spreading for miles underground.

The largest animal that has ever lived on our planet is still around: the blue whale. Because whales are so familiar to us, their sheer size is lost on us. But try to wrap your mind around these facts:

- An adult blue whale can grow to be a hundred feet long—the length of three school buses lined up end to end to end.
- Elephants are massive, but a blue whale's *tongue* weighs the same as a single adult elephant. Just the tongue! The entire whale? It can weigh more than two hundred tons!
- Blue whales have a heart the size of a compact car, and their blood vessels are so large a human could swim through them.
- The song of a blue whale can reach up to 180 decibels, which is louder than a jet engine! And that song can be heard a thousand miles away.

Isn't it amazing that the same God who created tiny ants and intricate hummingbirds also created the majestic creature we call a blue whale? Maybe God is telling us something through the world He created—through the creatures that swim and fly and crawl on this planet. Maybe He is introducing Himself through the variety and creativity of creation. Are we listening?

"Miracles are a retelling in small letters," said C. S. Lewis, "of the very same story which is written across the whole world in letters too large for some of us to see."[1]

Which animals fascinated you when you were growing up? Which ones inspired you to learn everything you could about them? What drove that fascination?

_____

_____

_____

What fascinates you now when you look around at the natural world? How have your interactions with that world broadened your understanding of God?

_____

_____

_____

STUDY THE WORDS

The world is filled with innumerable miracles gift wrapped for us by our Creator. One of those gifts is an endless opportunity to experience wonder.

Let's be honest: Day-to-day life can become a blur. The thing about daily routines is that, by definition, they can become routine! Day in and day out life can become drudgery. Busywork. Chores we assign ourselves simply because we think we're supposed to do them. It can get tiring trying to trudge through those checklists day after day after day.

The natural world is a gift because it helps us break free from that grind, even if only for a little while. A spectacular sunrise can wake us up to wonder. All of creation inspires us toward awe by reminding us that the Creator is awesome. The gifts we unwrap in nature reflect our Father, who gave them to us, and reflect His love for us.

Reread the story of Arthur Gordon and his two-foot field trip on pages 29–31 of A Million Little Miracles. *Did you ever experience something similar as a child or a teenager? Was there a moment when wonder invaded your life? Made time stand still? How did that experience affect your life?*

_____

_____

_____

If we aren't careful, our lives can gather the dust of daily drudgeries. We choose sleep over shooting stars. We all live under the same sky as Arthur Gordon and his father. What's keeping you from living your life the way they did? All it takes is a little intentionality.

Time is measured in minutes.

Life is measured in moments.

All that stands between you and a million little miracles is your capacity for wonder.

—MARK BATTERSON, *A Million Little Miracles*

How frequently do you experience the emotion of wonder?

1	2	3	4	5	6	7	8	9	10

(RARELY)   (DAILY)

How would you rate your capacity to experience wonder? How intensely do you react in the presence of something awesome?

1	2	3	4	5	6	7	8	9	10

(VERY LOW)   (VERY HIGH)

God's attributes are reflected in the world He created. The tenderness of a mother hen wrapping her chicks in the warmth of her wings is a reflection of God's tender love for His children. The majesty of a redwood forest mirrors the majesty of God. Even something as frightening as a terrific thunderstorm can reveal God's power. Fun fact? There are eight million lightning strikes every single day![2]

We rarely talk about another aspect of God's character displayed in nature. Though it's an attribute we appreciate as human beings, we don't usually connect it with God—we may even think it would be inappropriate to do so. What is it? *Playfulness.*

Have you seen videos of dolphins using a piece of seaweed to play tag? How about juvenile squirrels chasing each other up and down a tree, rushing up the bark and jumping from branch to branch? Have you ever seen a dog get the zoomies and go tearing around a living room like it just drank a double espresso? Our world is filled with playfulness, and the resulting joy is not in defiance of God but *because* of God. Part of spiritual maturity is a well-developed theology of fun.

Jesus pushed the playfulness envelope further than anyone. He said that we can't enter the kingdom of heaven
unless we become like little children,[3] and part of becoming like little children is recapturing what they are
best at—playfulness....

Theodor Geisel, better known as Dr. Seuss, said,
"Adults are obsolete children."[4] The good news? It's
never too late to become who you might have been. The
key? To become like Christ is to become like a little
child, and to become like a little child is to recapture the
sacredness of play. What kind of play? Anything you can
imagine! Play a game. Play an instrument. Play with
Legos. Just play!

—MARK BATTERSON, *A Million Little Miracles*

*What is your response to the concept of God being playful? How does
that idea hit you emotionally? Why?*

_____

_____

_____

*Think about the phrase "the sacredness of play." In your experience,
what benefits do we receive from playfulness and fun?*

_____

_____

_____

Let's talk about *tov*. It's a Hebrew word that's somewhat difficult to define because it's multidimensional. Scholars often

translate *tov* as "good." The first example? "God said, 'Let there be light,' and there was light. And God saw that the light was [*tov*]" (Genesis 1:3–4).

Tov does mean "good," but that falls short of its true essence. *Tov* is gooder than good. *Tov* is as good as it gets. Tov is too good to be true, yet it is! It's not limited to goodness in the way our culture defines it. Picture the most beautiful sight you've ever seen. That would be *tov*. Or think back to the most fun you've ever experienced in a single hour. That hour would be *tov*. The last time you were at a loss for words—so much so that you couldn't not worship—was also *tov*. Tov is joy unspeakable and peace that passes understanding.

This incredible idea, and all the emotions that go with it, is yet another gift God has given us through creation. And the way we steward that gift is by enjoying it!

> The first tenet of the Westminster Catechism states, "Man's chief end is to glorify God, and to enjoy him forever."[5] The first half makes perfect sense—creation exists to glorify the Creator. One way we do that is by co-creating with Him. The second half is less intuitive. Why? Because we've failed to connect enjoyment with original emotion. What if the first half of that tenet is fulfilled by the second half? God is most glorified in us when we delight in Him. We glorify God by enjoying God and all that He has made. We worship God by exploring, by naming, by stewarding, and, yes, by enjoying His creation.
>
> —MARK BATTERSON, *A Million Little Miracles*

As you consider the concept expressed by the word tov, *use the space below to draw a moment from your past that illustrates that concept—a moment when you experienced the extreme goodness God has baked into our world.*

[ ]

On a practical level, what does it mean to enjoy God or take delight in His goodness? What does that actually look like?

_____

_____

_____

STUDY GOD'S WORD

There's a tendency in our culture today—and even in the church—to think of the world in negative terms. It's a function of the negativity bias that infects and affects all of us. Watch the news for five minutes and you'll see reminders of the fallen world we live in—violence, corruption, pain, and suffering. If we're not careful, we can conclude that our world has always been a place from which God intended us to escape. That everything we will experience in heaven is right but everything we experience on earth is wrong.

But that's not true. The universe God created was inherently good. It was lovely and beautiful and fun because its Creator is lovely and beautiful and fun. Scripture tells us,

> God said, "Let us make human beings in our image, to be like us. They will reign over the fish in the sea, the birds in the sky, the livestock, all the wild animals on the earth, and the small animals that scurry along the ground."
>
> So God created human beings in his own image.
>   In the image of God he created them;
>   male and female he created them.
>
> Then God blessed them and said, "Be fruitful and multiply. Fill the earth and govern it. Reign over the fish in the sea, the birds in the sky, and all the animals that scurry along the ground."
> Then God said, "Look! I have given you every seed-bearing plant throughout the earth and all the fruit trees for your food. And I have given every green plant as food for all the wild animals, the birds in the sky, and the small animals that scurry along the ground—everything that has life." And that is what happened.
> Then God looked over all he had made, and he saw that it was very good!
>
> —GENESIS 1:26–31

What can we learn about humanity from these verses? What is our nature and purpose?

_____

_____

_____

What can we learn about God from these verses? Explore the rest of Genesis 1 as well. What did God reveal about Himself through creation?

_____

_____

_____

_____

Don't miss this: What God created is still *tov*. Our universe and everything in it—even our own humanity—is still "very good." Yes, that creation has been infected and corrupted by sin. But sin doesn't have the power to eliminate the goodness of God. His goodness still exists in everything He has touched, which, of course, is everything ever made. If you want to rediscover a million little miracles, a good place to start is common grace and common good.

If Adam and Eve hadn't sinned, would they have remained in the Garden of Eden forever? No. Our original mission was to "fill the earth and govern it." And that mission still remains! That opportunity is still right here in front of us. It doesn't mean we have to add stamps to our passports. It means praising God for every square inch of His creation, right where we are.

I'm certainly not implying that sin isn't a big deal. It is. But Jesus has taken care of the sin problem. Our sin is forgiven and forgotten by virtue of what He accomplished on the cross. As such, the whole world exists as a playground for us to encounter God, worship God, and do the work God has created us to do.

How do we fulfill our mission to "fill the earth and govern it"? What does that mean on a practical level? What does that mean for you?

_____

_____

_____

What are some reasons people associate fun with sin? What would it look like to connect fun with worship?

_____

_____

_____

CARPE WONDER

The apostle Paul said, "Whether you eat or drink, or whatever you do, do it all for the glory of God" (1 Corinthians 10:31). What we often overlook is the imperative included in that passage. It's a command. A nonnegotiable. You and I have been told that *whatever* we do, it should translate to worship. We can glorify God while hiking, snorkeling, or bird-watching.

Even fun stuff can be to the glory of God. News flash: God *loves* your laugh. And according to the writer of Proverbs, it does good like a medicine! A theology of fun doesn't mean we don't take God seriously. We most certainly do. But we don't take *ourselves* too seriously. The happiest, healthiest, and holiest people on the planet are often those who laugh at themselves the most.

Eating a well-prepared meal is an opportunity to glorify God. Playing a video game with your child is an opportunity to glorify God. Jogging across a white-sand beach is an opportunity to glorify God.

The question is, Are you taking advantage of those opportunities? Are you glorifying God by enjoying Him and enjoying His creation? God enjoys your enjoyment.

MY MIRACLES: *During this past week, how has God spoken to you or arrested your attention through fun and enjoyment? How has He offered to play with you? Write down any examples that come to mind.*

_____

_____

_____

What are some specific ways you are planning to have fun over the next few weeks or months? How can you connect those moments with the enjoyment of God?

_____

_____

_____

REMINDER: Read chapter 3 of *A Million Little Miracles* before engaging session 3 of this study guide.

FLATLAND

Based on chapter 3 of *A Million Little Miracles.*

START WITH A MIRACLE

Not many people have a scientific law named after them, but Edwin Hubble earned this distinction for good reason. In the 1920s, Hubble studied the light of distant galaxies and came to an astounding conclusion: They were expanding. Most astronomers at the time believed that the universe was fixed in place. The scientific consensus of Hubble's day held that the universe was static.

By exploring the redshift of the light reaching us from those distant galaxies, Hubble was able to prove that those galaxies were in fact not static. They were moving away from one another. And not just a few galaxies but all galaxies.

Hubble concluded that the universe is still expanding. He changed our fundamental understanding of the universe as a physical system, which means he changed the way we understand everything. And it's only getting more mysterious as some astrophysicists believe the universe may be expanding *faster* than the speed of light.[1]

All of that to say: Hubble's law offers incredible evidence for the existence of God. How so? If the universe is expanding in every direction like a balloon being inflated, that means we could theoretically rewind that expansion and return to a moment when the universe existed as a single point—as a single deflated balloon.

That moment would be the beginning of time and space, as we know it. And if there is a beginning to the universe, then there has to be something or Someone outside the universe that acted as a *Beginner.* Or, in the words of Thomas Aquinas, the *Unmoved Mover.*[2] Even more significant than developing the telescope named after him, Hubble provided us with evidence for the existence of God.

The supernatural reality of God's presence has been baked into the natural world, to infinity and beyond. The more we discover and discern that presence, the more we expand our own understanding.

When have you made a connection between Creator and creation that changed the way you see the world?

_____

_____

_____

_____

How would you describe the relationship between the scientific world and the spiritual world?

_____

_____

_____

STUDY THE WORDS

Our attempts to study God can be a bit of a catch-22. We can know God, but finite minds cannot know everything there is to

know about God. *Systematic theology* is an oxymoron if there ever
was one. Why? Because God works in strange and mysterious
ways! He is the same yesterday, today, and forever. That said,
God is predictably unpredictable!

All we've ever known is four dimensions of reality. Those four
dimensions are the water in which we swim. They are physical
and spiritual boundaries through which we experience everything. That becomes a problem when we think of God as a four-
dimensional Being. God exists on a completely different plane.
While we are limited by physical space, God is omnipresent. His
omniscience has no limits. We live in a very thin slice of reality
called the present, but God does not. He can interact with past,
present, and future simultaneously.

God is infinitely beyond our ability to comprehend, yet we
constantly try to engage with Him based on our own limits,
our own boundaries. Because we subconsciously impose those
limits and boundaries on everything we interact with, we de-
velop a very small view of who God is and what He can ac-
complish.

That is our biggest problem—our small view of God.

Faith is a many-splendored thing, so let me share a few
of my favorite definitions. Faith is taking the first step
before God reveals the second. If doubt is letting our circumstances get between us and God, faith is putting
God between us and our circumstances. Faith is the will-
ingness to look foolish. Faith is unlearning fear. Percep-
tually speaking, faith is seeing the invisible and hearing
the inaudible. Faith is a sixth sense—extrasensory
perception—that enables us to imagine realities beyond
what we can see, hear, taste, touch, and smell.

—MARK BATTERSON, *A Million Little Miracles*

Look again at the description of the book Flatland *on page 52 of* A Million Little Miracles. *How would you explain the concept being illustrated in the book? How does that concept relate to our understanding of God?*

Based on the above definitions of faith, when have you exercised faith in a major way? What happened next?

Let's consider what we know about miracles. To start, we typically think of a miracle as something that defies our understanding of what's possible. A woman healed of cancer without medical intervention. A child who survives a fall that should have been fatal and does so without a scratch. An addiction broken through the power of prayer. These are what many of us think of as miracles, and they most certainly qualify as such. But if we aren't careful, we discount everyday miracles by narrow framing miracles as only anomalies.

We often think of miracles as happening instantaneously, but that's not always the case. Sometimes God does miracles in stages. My advice? Praise God for partial miracles! God often dispenses His supernatural power over a period of time—with the Lord, a day is like a thousand years—to achieve His eternal purposes.

Remember the blind man from Bethsaida? Jesus laid hands on him once, and his vision improved, but it wasn't entirely restored. The miracles happened in stages! What if that man had walked away frustrated by that partial miracle? He would have forfeited the full miracle! It wasn't until Jesus touched his eyes a second time that the man was completely healed.

Every miracle is a moment in which God exercises His authority over creation—over what we would consider to be scientific laws. We marvel at such moments because we are bound to those laws of nature in our current state. But God is bound to nothing. Miracles remind us that He is sovereign over everything. They expand our understanding of His nature and character.

John's gospel records seven miracles that double as seven signs. Jesus turned water into wine, revealing His authority over the periodic table of elements. He healed a nobleman's son long distance, revealing His Lordship over latitude and longitude. When He healed a man who hadn't walked in thirty-eight years, He revealed Himself as the Time Lord. When He fed five thousand people with five loaves and two fish, He is Math Lord. Yes, I'm taking a little liberty with these names, but how else would you describe what He did? Jesus walked on water, defying the laws of physics. Jesus healed a man who was born blind, defying the laws of neuroanatomy. If you are born blind, there is no synaptic pathway between the optic nerve and visual cortex in the brain. This miracle is nothing short of synaptogenesis. Then Jesus raised a man who was four days dead with three words: "Lazarus, come forth."[3]

—MARK BATTERSON, *A Million Little Miracles*

Should followers of Jesus expect to witness miracles in our modern world? Explain your answer.

_____

_____

_____

Because we are "natural" and miracles are "supernatural," what role do we have in the process of miracles? Do we carry any responsibility when it comes to God's supernatural involvement in our world?

_____

_____

_____

Many people have a yes-or-no frame of mind when it comes to God's miraculous intervention in the world. Many Jesus followers believe miracles occur—just not to them. If you asked them whether God intervenes in the world to help His children, they would say yes. But if you asked whether they expect God to intervene miraculously on their behalf, they would say no.

One reason many people feel this way is that they view their problems, their issues, as too small for God's attention. Or they view *themselves* as too small or too unimportant for God's attention. Not true! God cares about the minute details of our lives. To believe anything less is to misunderstand the heart of the heavenly Father.

If we can wrap our minds around the reality that God is infinite—that He has no limits and no boundaries—then we will start to see that nothing is too small or too unimportant for His attention. He designed our universe, from the most massive galaxy all the way down to the smallest subatomic particle. Likewise, He has the capacity to involve Himself in the life of every person who has ever lived. Including you.

> Show me the size of your dream, and I'll show you the size of your God. God makes big people by giving them big dreams. Why? It keeps us on our knees! If God doesn't do it, it can't be done. And that way, when the miracle happens, we can't take credit. God gets all the glory! My advice? Go after a dream that is destined to fail without divine intervention.
>
> If God is for us, who can be against us?[4]
>
> The same Spirit that raised Christ from the dead dwells in us![5]
>
> I can do all things through Christ, who gives me strength.[6]
>
> —MARK BATTERSON, *A Million Little Miracles*

Where do you need God's intervention in your world right now? Where do you need a miracle?

_____

_____

_____

Take a moment to write down some of the dreams you are currently striving to achieve. What do those dreams reveal about your understanding of God and what He can achieve?

_____

_____

STUDY GOD'S WORD

The Old Testament is an incredible collection of ancient literature. It's got history, poetry, prophecy, and biography. One of the most important things we can glean from these books is how our view of God—big or small—plays out in real life.

Consider the story of the twelve spies. As you might remember, when the Israelites first reached the promised land, Moses sent twelve scouts to survey the land and do some reconnaissance work for Israel's military leaders. Ten of those spies had a small view of God:

> This was their report to Moses: "We entered the land you sent us to explore, and it is indeed a bountiful country—a land flowing with milk and honey. Here is the kind of fruit it produces. But the people living there are powerful, and their towns are large and fortified. We even saw giants there, the descendants of Anak! The Amalekites live in the Negev, and the Hittites, Jebusites, and Amorites live in the hill country. The Canaanites live along the coast of the Mediterranean Sea and along the Jordan Valley." . . .
>
> "We can't go up against them! They are stronger than we are!" So they spread this bad report about the land among the Israelites: "The land we traveled through and explored will devour anyone who goes to live there. All the people we saw were huge. We even saw giants there, the descendants of Anak. Next to them we felt like grasshoppers, and that's what they thought, too!"
>
> —NUMBERS 13:27–29, 31–33

Circle any words or phrases in this passage that hint at a small view of God. How did that view influence the way those ten spies saw the world?

_____

_____

_____

What are some characteristics of a person with a small view of God today? How does that view affect their life?

_____

_____

_____

In direct contrast to those ten spies were Joshua and Caleb. Those two men went on the same scouting mission, they saw the same giants, but because of their view of God, they provided a different report:

> Two of the men who had explored the land, Joshua son of Nun and Caleb son of Jephunneh, tore their clothing. They said to all the people of Israel, "The land we traveled through and explored is a wonderful land! And if the Lord is pleased with us, he will bring us safely into that land and give it to us. It is a rich land flowing with milk and honey. Do not rebel against the Lord, and don't be afraid of the people of the land. They are only helpless prey to us! They have no protection, but the Lord is with us! Don't be afraid of them!"
>
> —NUMBERS 14:6–9

Circle any words or phrases in this passage that hint at a large view of God. How did that view influence the way those two spies saw the world?

_____

_____

_____

What are some characteristics of a person with a large view of God today? How does that view affect their life?

_____

_____

_____

CARPE WONDER

We've been talking about faith throughout this session, which essentially means an ever-expanding view of God. According to A. W. Tozer, a *low view* of God is "the cause of a hundred lesser evils,"[7] while a *high view* of God is the solution to ten thousand problems.[8]

Like the universe, faith isn't static. It's always contracting or expanding. And we never reach a place where doubt is a thing of the past. It's important to remember that all of us experience doubt in different ways. Abraham doubted that God could give him a child in his old age. Moses doubted his ability to speak. David doubted God's presence a time or two or three. The prophets experienced doubt during Israel's exile. Even the disciples experienced doubt—and not just Thomas. All of them were card-carrying members of the Doubters' Club.

If there are elements of your spiritual life that cause you to feel doubt, join the club. You're in good company. Don't give up simply because you feel some doubt. My advice? Don't just doubt your faith, doubt your doubt. Use moments of doubt as opportunities to take a larger leap of faith. Trust is a choice! Choose to trust in God.

MY MIRACLES: *In recent months, when have you taken a step of faith? When have you done something specifically because you believed God would back you up? Write down even small examples that come to mind.*

Where do you have an opportunity right now to take a leap of faith? What would it look like to leap in a big way?

REMINDER: Read chapter 4 of *A Million Little Miracles* before engaging session 4 of this study guide.

HOLY CURIOSITY

Based on chapter 4 of *A Million Little Miracles*.

START WITH A MIRACLE

Did you know you're a cancer survivor? We all are. Every human being carries cells that have the potential to break free from our internal containment systems and produce life-threatening tumors. That's what's happening—whether you know it or not—throughout the many systems in your body this very moment.

You are under threat. That's the bad news. The good news? You are constantly protected by specialized white blood cells called T cells, aka natural killer T cells. These incredible cells are immunological assassins. More than a trillion T-cells guard your body day and night, physically patrolling your cells in search of cancerous rebels.

When a T cell discovers a cancerous cell, it latches on to the enemy's outer membrane and confirms specific chemical markers that are always present with cancer. The T cell then punctures the enemy's membrane and uses microtubules to deliver protein-based cytotoxins directly into the cell, killing it. T cells don't stop there, though. They continue to prowl that same area, looking for additional cancerous cells to be identified, tagged, and destroyed.

But here's the really crazy part: There are one million T cells in every milliliter of human blood.[1] That means you're walking around right now with a heroic army of deadly defenders—all highly trained and driven by a singular purpose: to keep you healthy.

Scripture says that life is in the blood.[2] So are a million little miracles! Flowing through your veins and arteries is evidence that the One who created you cares for you.

When have you been protected from sickness or blessed with healing in a way that felt meaningful?

Sometimes we don't experience healing, and other times we aren't protected from difficult circumstances. How can we reconcile those experiences with the reality of God's love?

STUDY THE WORDS

You and I have a lot to be grateful for, and little miracles like T cells are just the beginning. Every breath is an opportunity for gratitude. Every heartbeat is an opportunity for gratitude. Every sound wave that drums against the tympanic membrane of our inner ear, every time light hits the photoreceptors inside our eyes—those are opportunities for gratitude.

Fun fact? More than half the human body is *not* human.[3] Wait, what? More than half of the human body consists of microscopic microbes that make up our microbiome, and they are absolutely essential to good health. When was the last time your praised God for the billions of bacteria that help you digest food?

Gratitude includes giving thanks for things we did nothing to deserve, but that doesn't mean it's effortless. Gratitude is a muscle that has to be exercised or it atrophies. We must shift our focus from what's *wrong* to what's *right*. We have to consciously make a decision *not* to complain about all the things that seem to be going wrong or all the circumstances that cause stress. Instead, we must focus on all the wonderful things that are going well. That is our ticket to wonderland, and it's free ninety-nine. Though it may come more naturally to some people, gratitude requires an active effort.

Thankfully, the benefits are worth the effort. Cultivating gratitude in our lives is a guaranteed method to becoming happier, healthier, and holier. When we increase our capacity for gratitude, it increases our ability to see the million little miracles at work around us and in us.

Did you know that gratitude and anxiety can't coexist in the human mind?[4] There is something about gratitude that flips the switch on anxiety. If you increase gratitude, you decrease anxiety by default. Gratitude puts us into a parasympathetic state, which releases dopamine and serotonin. Gratitude is the difference between fight-or-flight and rest-and-recovery.

In part 1, we counted stars. While you're at it, count your blessings! But don't stop counting once you've listed all the obvious ones. Keep digging deeper and deeper. Remember how God ended each day of creation? He paused and took joy in His creation. What if you set aside a few minutes at the end of the day to count your blessings? It might not change your circumstances, but I guarantee it would change *you*! After you count your blessings, flip those blessings for other people, and gratitude will grow like compound interest.

—MARK BATTERSON, *A Million Little Miracles*

Use the space that follows to write down as many reasons for gratitude as you can think of in the next three minutes. What emotions do you experience as you count your blessings?

_____

_____

_____

When could you set aside time each day to focus on what you are grateful for? Consider starting a gratitude journal. What could that look like, and what obstacles would you need to overcome to record something in it each day?

_____

_____

_____

Here's another big benefit of gratitude: It's the key that opens the door to praise. The more we pay attention to the myriad miracles surrounding us, the more opportunities we have to be caught up in worship. After all, every single miracle is praiseworthy!

Remember when Jesus was in the region of Sidon and He healed a man with a speech impediment? Scripture says, "Jesus led him away from the crowd so they could be alone" (Mark 7:33). He was seeking a little privacy for this specific healing. However, the disappearing act didn't work, because a crowd witnessed the event. Jesus urged the man and the crowd not to talk about what had happened. Why? Because Jesus didn't want to reveal His identity as the Messiah just yet, knowing He was on a collision course with the Pharisees.

His attempts to keep things quiet didn't work. "The more he told them not to, the more they spread the news" (verse 36).

Shouldn't that be us? How can we remain silent about the wonders of God? About the miracles we experience each day? We should shout our praise from the rooftops!

> Orthodox Jews pronounce a minimum of a hundred blessings a day, which is quite the quota. Those blessings cover the gamut of human experience, but their breadth is matched by their depth. A blessing is spoken *before* and *after* enjoying a meal, as well as *during* the meal. Freshly baked bread, for example, is a double blessing. The smell and taste are two separate blessings! And if it's fresh out of the oven, add a third blessing for melted butter. Add a fourth blessing for a dash of Himalayan salt. If you want to push the gratitude envelope even further, praise God for each of the ingredients in the bread.
>
> "A man embezzles from God," says the Talmud, "when he makes use of this world without uttering a blessing."[5] Again, if we don't take things for gratitude, we take them for granted. And if we take them for granted, it's as if we've stolen them from God. That's why identifying everyday miracles—and praising God for them—is at the core of spiritual growth.
>
> —MARK BATTERSON, *A Million Little Miracles*

How often do you give thanks to God during a typical day? What causes you to praise Him?

_____

_____

_____

What are some reasons we find it so easy to "embezzle from God"? What obstacles prevent us from praising Him?

_____

_____

_____

I'm grateful for the Bible. We can open the pages of Scripture—anytime, anywhere—and read the very words of God. The same God who created the universe also conceived of you. The same God who has authority over the four fundamental forces has plans and purposes for your life—right down to ordering your footsteps. And we can access the wisdom of God any moment we choose by opening Scripture. When was the last time you thanked God for His Word?

Scripture is *special* revelation, but there is a second type of revelation—*natural* revelation, or *general* revelation. Simply put, the Creator has revealed Himself through creation. He has left creation clues. Not only can we encounter God through the Bible, but we can also encounter Him by making angels in freshly fallen snow, tasting the salt of ocean waves, and hearing the song of the mockingbird outside our window.

In the words of Paul, "Ever since the world was created, people have seen the earth and sky. Through everything God made, they can clearly see his invisible qualities—his eternal power and divine nature" (Romans 1:20).

> My point? A walk through the woods can turn into a ticker-tape parade of praise. A visit to the botanical gardens can raise the roof in worship. An ordinary hike can turn into a two-foot field trip that changes your perspective on life and love and leadership.
>
> When C. S. Lewis was a young boy, his brother handed him a biscuit tin filled with moss and decorated with twigs and flowers. That simple little garden toy elicited what Lewis called a "stab of Joy." He found himself overwhelmed with a profound longing for something he couldn't quite name. That biscuit tin became holy ground. It was the beginning of a lifelong search for the Source of that joy! "The central story of my life," said Lewis, "is about nothing else."[6]
>
> —MARK BATTERSON, *A Million Little Miracles*

When have you experienced a "stab of Joy" from the natural world? What happened next?

_____

_____

_____

Why is it helpful to have both general revelation (the natural world) and specific revelation (the Bible) as a means for encountering God? What would we lose if one of those sources was missing?

_____

_____

STUDY GOD'S WORD

Holy curiosity is one of the most spiritual traits we can cultivate in our lives. It's the ability to experience the world with a child-like wonder. It's the resolve not to take things at face value. It's digging deeper by asking questions. It's investigating. It's exploring. It's engaging the world with a growth mindset, a learning posture.

In many ways, Solomon was the patron saint of holy curiosity. He was interested in *everything*! Birds, insects, food, populations, principles, poetry, and more. As a result, he became captivated by the miracles all around him. Here is a sampling from Proverbs:

The way of the righteous is like the first gleam of dawn,
    which shines ever brighter until the full light of day.
But the way of the wicked is like total darkness.
    They have no idea what they are stumbling over.
                                                —4:18–19

Take a lesson from the ants, you lazybones.
    Learn from their ways and become wise!
Though they have no prince
    or governor or ruler to make them work,
they labor hard all summer,
    gathering food for the winter.
                                                —6:6–8

The seeds of good deeds become a tree of life;
    a wise person wins friends.
                                                —11:30

Without oxen a stable stays clean,
> but you need a strong ox for a large harvest.

—14:4

How would you summarize the lesson or principle communicated by each of these proverbs?

_____

_____

_____

How do these proverbs reflect Solomon's holy curiosity?

_____

_____

_____

Solomon's intense study of the world around him provided more than intellectual stimulation. It gave him opportunities to worship God. His dedication to holy curiosity was both a spur and a springboard for his spiritual life.

In Psalm 72, Solomon expressed his desire for God's blessings as he carried out the duties of the kingship. Notice how Solomon ended that song—with a burst of praise:

Praise the LORD God, the God of Israel,
> who alone does such wonderful things.
Praise his glorious name forever!
> Let the whole earth be filled with his glory.
Amen and amen!

—VERSES 18–19

Take a moment to read Psalm 72 in its entirety. Where do you see evidence of Solomon's holy curiosity?

_____

_____

_____

What does God receive or gain when we offer Him glory and praise? What do we receive?

_____

_____

_____

CARPE WONDER

Followers of Jesus should be the last people on earth to embezzle the blessings we've received from God. We should be the first to praise God for our blessings by expressing genuine gratitude. Why? Because we've got inside information. We know the Source of every good thing we encounter each day.

The apostle James told us, "Whatever is good and perfect is a gift coming down to us from God our Father, who created all the lights in the heavens" (James 1:17). So let's keep an eye open for those good and perfect gifts. In fact, let's keep both eyes open! And let's never neglect an opportunity to thank God and praise Him for all He continues to provide.

MY MIRACLES: *During the past week, how has God reminded you of His goodness and provision in your life? How has God winked at you, even in a little way?*

_____

_____

_____

What is something you can do to remind yourself to be grateful each morning and each evening? How can you build that habit into your daily routine?

_____

_____

_____

REMINDER: Read chapter 5 of *A Million Little Miracles* before engaging session 5 of this study guide.

SLEEPING BEAUTIES

Based on chapter 5 of *A Million Little Miracles.*

START WITH A MIRACLE

Did you know scientists are working on a cure for blindness? Not just working on it—they're making significant progress. A novel method for treatment is based on the CRISPR gene-editing technology.[1] Believe it or not, we've reached the stage in scientific development where researchers are fighting disease by tweaking our genetic material!

Are there ethical implications? Absolutely. But advances in medicine are pretty amazing. Subjects in clinical trials have had very limited vision for most of their lives, but they have experienced significant improvement thanks to this new treatment.

Think about how their quality of life could change in real and practical ways. Imagine them seeing the faces of their parents or their children for the first time. Eyesight would enable them to read books, play *Candy Crush,* and FaceTime with loved ones. They could enjoy sunsets. And wildflowers. And mountain views.

What a miracle! But don't miss the forest for the trees. We shouldn't have to lose our eyesight to appreciate it. The fact that we can see—that we've always been able to see—is no less a miracle. Our pupils and retinas and optic nerves are miraculous. They enable us to visually process the world. We can enjoy the beauty of creation and the beauty of one another.

Sight is a miracle we dare not take for granted.

When was the last time you thanked God for depth perception or peripheral vision? How about color vision or panoramic vision?

Imagine if you had to live for a week without eyesight. What would be the biggest consequences of losing the ability to see, even temporarily? What would you be most excited to see again when your vision was restored?

Vision is just one way we perceive the world around us. On a scale of 1 (low) to 10 (high), how perceptive do you consider yourself? Think more than just visually. Explain.

STUDY THE WORDS

Many different camps exist within the scientific community. There are disagreements, big and little, about methods of study, sources of funding, and which models best explain the fundamentals of the universe. Science is done by scientists, and scientists are people. So the schisms within science are to be expected.

As you might imagine, one of the biggest disagreements among scientists revolves around the existence of God. The originator of the scientific method, Francis Bacon, certainly believed in God. But can the scientific method be employed to understand the supernatural? Many scientists would say no. Some scientists restrict their study to natural phenomena and the resulting data. Other scientists disagree, believing that if a Creator has played a role in the formation of our universe, it would be foolish to completely ignore that possibility.

As someone who believes in intelligent design, I side with the second group. One of the reasons God created the universe was to reveal Himself—to make Himself known. Imagine studying music without any knowledge of the musician. It seems silly to study a work of art without any knowledge of the artist. If there is a Creator, then ignoring Him seems, well, ignorant. I have a core conviction that every ology is a branch of theology.

Some fraction of the shaming and blaming that are happening in our culture, in my opinion, is the result of being spoon-fed a steady diet of Darwinism, which denies ultimate accountability to a Creator. You can't prove or disprove intelligent design, but intelligent design makes more sense than some scientists are willing to admit. Even if you don't believe in a Creator, you still need a cosmological starting point.

"Let's be scientifically honest," said Sir Fred Hoyle, the scientist who coined the term *big bang*. "The probability of life arising to greater and greater complexity by chance through evolution is the same probability as having a tornado tear through a junk yard and form a Boeing 747 jetliner."[2]

Life doesn't come from non-life.

—MARK BATTERSON, *A Million Little Miracles*

How does science help us recognize everyday miracles in our world?

_____

_____

_____

How does science unintentionally influence us to ignore a million little miracles in our world?

_____

_____

_____

God created us with two eyes to enjoy the visual panorama of our world, but that's not all He designed. We've also got two ears with which we can perceive the melodies of the universe. Sight and sound go together like peanut butter and jelly. In the words of Solomon, "Ears to hear and eyes to see—both are gifts from the LORD" (Proverbs 20:12).

The miracle of hearing gives us a sound bite into the worshipful nature of nature. Every hum of an insect wing is a song of praise to the Creator of all things. Every firefly that flashes, every frog that croaks, every cricket that chirps is the call of the wild. Our ears allow us to perceive and participate in that great chorus of praise.

Speaking of, the gift of sound allows us to make a joyful noise unto the Lord. What a privilege! What a wonder! When we worship, we are harmonizing with heaven. What's *really* happening in heaven right now? Angels and elders and living creatures are singing, "Holy, holy, holy is the Lord God, the Almighty—the one who always was, who is, and who is still to come" (Revelation 4:8).

Few things are more cathartic, more catalytic than worship. Why? Because that's what we were created to do.
You can't *not* worship. Either you will worship God with
a capital *G,* or you will substitute a lesser god. Not only
does worship improve vagal tone, but it also gets us on
God's wavelength. It helps us discern the still small voice
of the Spirit. It activates the gifts of the Spirit, as well as
prophetic imagination.

—MARK BATTERSON, *A Million Little Miracles*

*How would you explain the difference between singing and
worship? What transforms the former into the latter?*

_____

_____

_____

*Beyond singing, what are some ways we can express worship and
praise to God?*

_____

_____

_____

Our world is filled with wonders. We are surrounded by
sights and sounds that reflect God's goodness. We have opportunities to see His glory every day. There are countless occasions
for us to join the chorus of praise that is so baked into creation
that even the rocks cry out.

But all too often, we miss those opportunities. We fail to hear
the chorus that creation is singing, because we've got AirPods in

our ears. We neglect to lift our voices unless we're gathered in a sanctuary on Sunday morning. Why? Because we get distracted. We're so focused on other things—the emails that need to be sent, the bills that need to be paid, the weeds that need to be pulled, the meals that need to be cooked, the creaky joint in our knee that needs to get checked out—that we miss the miracle.

We allow the burdens of life to limit our capacity for wonder.

It was a cold winter night—so cold you could see your breath. My grandpa was carrying me in his arms as we walked through a tree farm, hunting for the perfect Douglas fir. There were no clouds in the sky, so the stars were shining extra bright. Maybe that's what prompted my grandpa to quote Psalm 19: "The heavens declare the glory of God."[3] Those words, spoken that night, are etched into my memory. . . .

In Greek and Latin, the etymology of the word for "wonder" is the same as the word for "miracle."[4] They are two sides of the same coin. If you want to recapture childlike wonder, it starts with rediscovering everyday miracles. *Sacramental* is the combination of two words— *sacred* and *mental*. We sacramentalize the world when we keep the sacred in mind.

—MARK BATTERSON, *A Million Little Miracles*

When was the last time you were overwhelmed with wonder because of God's power or beauty revealed through creation? How did you respond?

One of the main goals of this study is to capture the reality of everyday miracles. What have you encountered from the study so far that is helping you do that? What obstacles still need to be overcome?

STUDY GOD'S WORD

Do you remember Bezalel? He was the first person described in Scripture as being filled with the Holy Spirit. He wasn't a priest or a prophet or a public figure. He was a creative who God commissioned to help construct the tabernacle.

What does that say about God? The Creator loves creatives! And evidently, they are key when it comes to the kingdom of God.

> The LORD said to Moses, "Look, I have specifically chosen Bezalel son of Uri, grandson of Hur, of the tribe of Judah. I have filled him with the Spirit of God, giving him great wisdom, ability, and expertise in all kinds of crafts. He is a master craftsman, expert in working with gold, silver, and bronze. He is skilled in engraving and mounting gemstones and in carving wood. He is a master at every craft!
>
> "And I have personally appointed Oholiab son of Ahisamach, of the tribe of Dan, to be his assistant. Moreover, I have given special skill to all the gifted craftsmen so they can make all the things I have commanded you to make."
>
> —EXODUS 31:1–6

Read through Exodus 36–38 to see Bezalel and Oholiab at work. What are some specific artistic touches or expressions you find most interesting from those chapters? Why?

_____

_____

_____

How would you describe the connection between artistic expression and worshipping God? How do those concepts feed into each other?

_____

_____

_____

Don't underestimate the law of first mention. The first infilling of the Spirit unleashed creativity in Bezalel. This is a verse we pay little attention to in the church today: "I have filled him with the Spirit of God, giving him great wisdom, ability, and expertise in all kinds of crafts."

The Holy Spirit didn't fill Bezalel so that he could lead an army or confront injustice or preach a sermon. The anointing is for all people, for all things. And that certainly includes creative endeavors.

I know people who say they aren't creative. Truth be told? All of us are creative when it comes to making excuses! The potential for creativity is there, but it has to be channeled in the right way.

God anointed Bezalel for the express purpose of art. Is it possible that art is a form of apologetics? Our creativity is evidence of a Creator, just as imagination is an expression of His image. God wanted His tabernacle to be a beautiful expression of color and texture. A visual feast. A work of art. Twelve chapters in Exodus are devoted to the aesthetics of the tabernacle. The Holy Spirit inspired artists to help generations of Israelites worship through the tabernacle and, later, through the temple.

What kinds of hands-on experiences do you enjoy? What would it look like to transform those experiences into worship?

_____

_____

_____

What are some ways churches historically have incorporated visual expression as an act of worship? How do we do that today?

_____

_____

_____

CARPE WONDER

We've got eyes to see and ears to hear, and both are gifts from our Father, who loves us. Both are windows through which we perceive Him and express our own devotion to Him. Light and sound. Seeing and hearing. These are incredible miracles.

This week, make it a point to stop neglecting these gifts and start stewarding them. Keep your eyes open as you look for glimpses of God's beauty reflected in creation. Keep your ears open as you listen for sounds that double as songs. Then use your voice to give Him praise.

MY MIRACLES: *During the past week, what are some of the most beautiful things you've witnessed? What steps can you take to praise God in those moments of seeing His loveliness?*

_____

_____

_____

What songs or sounds do you most associate with worship right now? What can you do to experience them more frequently?

_____

_____

_____

REMINDER: Read chapter 6 of *A Million Little Miracles* before engaging session 6 of this study guide.

CONSIDER THE LILIES

Based on chapter 6 of *A Million Little Miracles*.

START WITH A MIRACLE

Around the year 1590, a young man named Zacharias Janssen invented the microscope. Janssen was an eyeglass maker at the time—an apprentice to his father, Hans—so he was quite familiar with lenses. As is often the case when it comes to innovation, Janssen adapted the familiar technology in such a way that he could see objects magnified at ten times their normal appearance.

Several decades later, a Dutch scientist named Antonie van Leeuwenhoek adapted the Janssen microscope, upgrading it in several key ways. Those modifications resulted in a microscope that could magnify objects up to *270 times* their normal appearance. It proved to be a small step and giant leap in microscopy.

It's difficult to overstate how incredible these advancements were in the scientific community. Prior to Janssen, we could see only what we could see—what was observable with the naked eye. We could squint, but that was about it. With the advent of the microscope came a whole new world. Human tissue could be studied under magnification, revealing the secrets of our cells. Bacteria became visible for the first time. Microscopes were critical in the development of germ theory, which had innumerable implications for the science of medicine.

Zacharias Janssen opened the door to an entirely new world.

Then Van Leeuwenhoek opened it a little wider. What was inaccessible was now accessible. What was invisible was now observable. What used to be completely mysterious was now understood.

History is filled with everyday miracles we call technology. But few inventions changed the way we do science more than the microscope. It radically altered the way we look at the world, giving us the ability to see what had been invisible for most of human history.

On a scale of 1 (low) to 10 (high), how would you rate your ability to concentrate on a specific object or idea and study it in detail? Overall, how would you rate your ability to focus?

_____

_____

_____

How could you improve your focus? How might doing so help you grow in your relationship with God?

_____

_____

_____

STUDY THE WORDS

There is an old axiom: *Seeing is believing.* That's true, but so is the opposite—*believing is seeing.* The ability to see is a miracle, in and of itself, but sometimes just seeing isn't enough. We have to learn more to see more. We have to cultivate mindfulness via meditation. To linger instead of just looking. To study instead of just seeing.

Our world is filled with incredible opportunities for worship and wonder—opportunities we'll miss if we're not looking for them. If we stop at merely seeing, we miss dimensions of God's gifts. Remember Moses and the burning bush? He saw it, and then he turned aside from what he was doing. He chose to step in and look closer. Then, and only then, did God speak through the bush, which was a seminal moment in Moses's life.

Make it a priority to stop and smell the roses—then study them. Focus long enough to discover what they can teach you. If something piques your curiosity, pause. That's part of what it means to be still and know that God is God. That's the heart of holy curiosity.

Read about Louis Agassiz on pages 120–22 of A Million Little Miracles. *Do you think this kind of deep study and intentional observation is helpful for all people, or is it just for scientists? Explain.*

There are a million little miracles hiding in plain sight. Of that I'm sure. But we must "learn to look" from different angles! When we do, we see new dimensions of who God is. "His science was infused with the presence of the divine," said Christoph Irmscher, "which he found wherever he went: in Swiss glaciers, American lakes, and the Amazonian rain forest."[1] Agassiz saw it as "missionary work of the highest order."[2]

There are naturalists who seem to look upon the idea of creation—that is, a manifestation of the intellectual power by material means—as a kind of bigotry; forgetting, no doubt, that whenever they carry out a thought of their own, they do something akin to creating.[3]

—MARK BATTERSON, *A Million Little Miracles*

Take a moment to attempt a brief version of Agassiz's fish experiment. Find something commonplace around you, and spend the next five minutes looking at it from all angles. What do you observe about that object? What do you learn about it?

_____

_____

_____

There is a concept in science called *critical realism*. We can never know everything there is to know, which requires us to hold our theories humbly. There's a lot we know about the world, but there's much more we don't know. And we don't know what we don't know! In other words, there's always something new to discover.

The same is true of the human mind. We know a lot about the three pounds of gray matter that are housed safely within the cranium. We know about neurons and neurotransmitters. Our neuroanatomy is being mapped and remapped. But when it comes to the potential of our minds, we're just scratching the surface. We don't even fully understand what causes a brain freeze when we gulp down a Slurpee too quickly!

I believe the most amazing feature of the human mind is imagination. The metacognitive ability to interact with abstract ideas in real time is nothing short of incredible. I'm blown away by our capacity to conceive of concepts previously unimagined.

You're probably familiar with the phrase *Cogito, ergo sum*—"I think; therefore, I am." A biblical rephrasing of that concept could be "I imagine; therefore, I will always be." Our imaginations are a reflection of the *imago Dei* inside us. It is one proof of our divine design and a unique connection to the Creator.

> Imagination is not just part of the image of God, but it's also the quintessence. As such, it's a superpower unique to humankind. Animals have hoarding instincts, but there is a big difference between storing acorns for winter and building skyscrapers. Humans split atoms and design computers. Humans write poems, compose music, and produce films. It's our God-given imagination that powers everything from rockets to romance. It's imagination that allows us to break through eight-foot ceilings.
> —MARK BATTERSON, *A Million Little Miracles*

What are some of the ways your ability to think and imagine has shaped your life?

Based on your understanding, what does it mean that human beings are created in God's image? What are the practical outworkings of that reality?

We explored two methods of perception in the last session: seeing and hearing. Now let's focus for a moment on the incredible blessing of physical touch. What would we be without that gift? What would life be like without sensory input from our fingertips, our taste buds, and the skin on the back of our neck?

Life would be a lot less lifelike—that's for sure. The ability to touch is a huge part of our lived experience. The solidity of the floor under our feet or the chair beneath our butt puts the real in reality. Touch keeps us connected to the physical world in ways that are hard to express but difficult to do without.

Our connection to the physical world via touch is valuable, but it pales in comparison with our connection to other people. In the beginning, God said, "It is not good for the man to be alone" (Genesis 2:18). Part of the reason is touch. When we are isolated, our senses suffer side effects. That's why solitary confinement is such a severe sentence. We were designed for close contact. The opportunity to enjoy the physical presence of friends and family—even co-workers and acquaintances—is yet another gift that reflects the triune community of our Creator.

> Loneliness is epidemic these days. Even in a crowd, some of us feel so alone. . . . The prescription for loneliness hasn't changed since the writer of Hebrews penned these words: "Let us not neglect our meeting together."[4] There is a supernatural synergy when two people pray together, when a small group gathers, when a congregation worships God corporately. The transformational power of community is one of God's most life-giving miracles—don't miss it. . . .
>
> Don't underestimate the power of a single touch. A hug has the power to change someone's life like it did

mine. There are very few miracles more amazing than touch, and God has put that miracle at our fingertips!

—MARK BATTERSON, *A Million Little Miracles*

God is a spiritual Being, yet He blessed us with physical bodies and the physical awareness we call touch. How does your ability to touch the world influence your relationship with God?

_____

_____

_____

How do you prefer to relate with others in a physical way? (For example, are you a hugger?) What are some symptoms that reveal that our need for physical touch isn't being met?

_____

_____

_____

STUDY GOD'S WORD

One of the most poignant moments in the New Testament is the healing of a woman who had suffered from bleeding for twelve years. According to Levitical law, this woman's bleeding made her ceremonially unclean. She couldn't worship at the temple. She couldn't participate in many elements of ordinary life. And—very importantly—she was forbidden to touch anyone while she was in this unclean state. That included the hem of Jesus's garment.

And that's what made her actions so shocking:

A woman in the crowd had suffered for twelve years with constant bleeding, and she could find no cure. Coming up behind Jesus, she touched the fringe of his robe. Immediately, the bleeding stopped.

"Who touched me?" Jesus asked.

Everyone denied it, and Peter said, "Master, this whole crowd is pressing up against you."

But Jesus said, "Someone deliberately touched me, for I felt healing power go out from me." When the woman realized that she could not stay hidden, she began to tremble and fell to her knees in front of him. The whole crowd heard her explain why she had touched him and that she had been immediately healed. "Daughter," he said to her, "your faith has made you well. Go in peace."

—LUKE 8:43–48

What do we risk in our modern world when we reach out to connect with Jesus? What do we risk when we reach out to try to connect with others?

_____

_____

_____

What have you lost or gained because of physical touch? How did it help or hurt you? In your opinion, why is appropriate physical touch so important?

_____

_____

_____

Beyond her desire for physical healing, this woman was desperate to be reintegrated into the community she had been ostracized from. Her ailment had separated her from that community. It had separated her from nearly every aspect of what we would consider normal relationships. I can't help but wonder how long it had been since she had been hugged.

Unfortunately, many people in our world today are suffering from something similar. Not physical bleeding but relational bleeding—the loss of community. According to the Census Bureau, I live in the loneliest city in the country: Washington, DC.[5] But loneliness is an epidemic all over the world. Despite advances in technology, many people feel more disconnected than ever. They see themselves as living on the outside looking in. They've lost touch with themselves because they've lost touch with others.

As followers of Jesus, we can invite them in—invite them into relationship, into community, and into the church. Many people need to feel like they *belong* before they believe. What stops us from taking advantage of that opportunity? What stops us from reaching out, as Jesus did, and touching those who long for the connection they were designed to enjoy?

Where do you see evidence of loneliness and disconnection in our world today? What about in your life?

What traumas or trials have held you back from reaching out to people who are longing for connection? What have you done to begin overcoming those obstacles?

_____

_____

_____

CARPE WONDER

Page 120 of *A Million Little Miracles* describes an assignment given to a student named Nathaniel Southgate Shaler. The professor gave Shaler a specimen jar with a fish inside and told him to study it until he had observed everything that could be seen. Shaler ended up studying the fish for ten hours a day over the course of two weeks. He was astonished by everything he observed.

Spend a few moments performing that experiment with yourself as the subject. Look into a mirror for ten minutes, studying yourself from all angles. Why? Because many of us are blind to ourselves. See if this experience doesn't heighten your self-awareness, which is part of the metacognitive capacity God has given us. Then use the prompts below to write down what you learn.

MY MIRACLES: *What did you observe about yourself that was new or interesting? Be specific, and write as many examples as you are able. What surprised you about this experience? Why?*

_____

_____

_____

Scripture describes us as the image of God, the apple of God's eye, and God's workmanship. Do you see yourself that way? If not, why not?

Sell your books at World of Books!
Go to sell.worldofbooks.com and get an instant price quote. We even pay the shipping - see what your old books are worth today!

Inspected By: maria_vargas2

00084208403

0008420 **8403** c-?

S-3

Did this experiment, do those verses of Scripture, change the way you see yourself?

_____

_____

_____

REMINDER: Read chapter 7 of *A Million Little Miracles* before engaging session 7 of this study guide.

GOOD GOD

Based on chapter 7 of *A Million Little Miracles*.

START WITH A MIRACLE

It's got to be one of the most unexpected gifts ever given. When Dr. Ruth Gottesman lost her husband, she was surprised to discover that he had been an early investor in Berkshire Hathaway. Her husband left her a huge stock portfolio that she had no idea existed.

But that's not the gift I'm talking about. At the age of ninety-three, Dr. Gottesman wanted to invest her money in a way that would make a difference not for a day, not for a year, not even for a lifetime—but for generations. So she donated a billion dollars to the Albert Einstein College of Medicine in the Bronx.[1]

Yep, a billion.

Her instructions were that the gift should be used to cover tuition for students. Not just current students but all future students as well. Imagine being a student at that college. You'd planned on financing your education through student loans, but when you go to pay back hundreds of thousands of dollars in debt, you learn that all your tuition has been covered for your entire education. No loans. No debt.

What a gift from Dr. Gottesman! What an expression of *goodness*. It reminds me of common grace—a free gift to everyone, everywhere, for all time. Remember the Hebrew word *tov*? That's what we're going to explore in the final three sessions of this study. We've seen in earlier sessions that God is bigger than big and closer than close. But is He good? That is *the* question. The answer? God is gooder than good. God is the definition of all that is good and true and beautiful.

Who are some people in your life who represent or radiate goodness? What is it about their actions or attitudes that affected your life? How did they leave their fingerprints on your soul?

_____

_____

_____

In your own words, when we identify God as good, what comes to mind? What does that mean?

_____

_____

_____

STUDY THE WORDS

What's the first thing we do when we meet someone? We learn their name: "Hi, I'm Mark. What's your name?" Our names are important as identifiers, but they don't really communicate who we are. They might reveal something about gender and culture, but that's become less certain in recent years. That said, the act of sharing our names is a vital point of connection. It's the first step in a potential pathway to relationship.

It's not surprising, then, that God uses the Bible to introduce Himself by introducing His names. It's part of His progressive revelation. The names of God are incredibly significant because they reveal His nature and character. Consider:

- *Elohim* means "God the Creator."
- *El Shaddai* is "God Almighty."
- *Adonai* is "Lord."
- *Jehovah Rapha* is "God our Healer."[2]
- *Jehovah Jireh* is "God our Provider."[3]
- *Jehovah Tsidkenu* is "God our Righteousness."

The priestly blessing is a powerful pronouncement: "The LORD bless you and keep you." But it's the postscript that packs the punch: "They will put my name on the Israelites, and I will bless them."[4] How do you put a name on someone? It's the same word used to describe putting on clothes or putting a ring on someone's finger.

When we put our faith in Christ, God does more than forgive and forget our sin. The righteousness of Christ is transferred to our account.[5] How much of it? All of it. God puts His name—Jehovah Tsidkenu—on us! You, my friend, are the righteousness of Christ.

—MARK BATTERSON, *A Million Little Miracles*

There is only one God, but there are as many as 967 names for God in Scripture.[6] *Take a moment to research some of the names, and write down those that are most meaningful to you. What makes those names captivating, encouraging, or awe-inspiring?*

_____

_____

_____

What names or titles do you typically use to address God or talk about Him? How do those names reflect your relationship with Him?

The names of God reveal His character, including His goodness. When God introduced Himself to Moses, for example, He declared Himself as "I AM WHO I AM" (Exodus 3:14), which can also be translated "I will be who I will be." God declared Himself to be immutable. His goodness doesn't change like shifting shadows. It remains the same yesterday, today, and forever.

Jesus reflected that goodness in the Gospels. He is described as full of grace and truth.[7] In the gospel of John, the apostle placed special emphasis on the seven times Jesus used "I am" statements to declare His nature and purpose:

- I am the Bread of Life.
- I am the Light of the World.
- I am the Door.
- I am the Vine.
- I am the Good Shepherd.
- I am the Resurrection and the Life.
- I am the Way, the Truth, and the Life.[8]

These aren't generic descriptors. They reveal Jesus *to* us and *for* us.

"Jesus is the dictionary," said Eugene Peterson, "in which we look up the meaning of words."[9] Jesus is "the image

of the invisible God, the firstborn over all creation."[10]
Jesus is the embodiment of grace and truth.[11] Jesus is the
definition of all that is good in the world.

   Jesus is the answer to every question.
   Jesus is the solution to every problem.
   Jesus is the fulfillment of every promise.
                    —MARK BATTERSON, *A Million Little Miracles*

*What are some of the ways we define Jesus based on our own
experiences or even on our own nature and character? Why is that
dangerous?*

_____

_____

_____

*How have you experienced Jesus in ways that align with the seven "I
Am" statements above? Be as specific as you can.*

_____

_____

_____

   Why is it so important to understand who God is? For start-
ers, if you misunderstand who God is, you'll relate to Him for all
the wrong reasons. Plus, *your* identity is based on God's identity.
After all, you were created in His image. You are described over
and over again in Scripture as His child.[12] If you're a follower of
Jesus, you're a temple of the Holy Spirit. The same Spirit that
raised Christ from the dead dwells in you!

   The goodness of Almighty God dwells within you. His character should be reflected in the way you live, the choices you make, and the person you present to the world. That's a reasonable expectation because you are created in the image of *tov,* of goodness.

Many people think that salvation is something to be earned by good works, but this is impossible. Thankfully, salvation is a gift. God made Him who knew no sin to become sin for us! Why? So that we might become the righteousness of Christ. "The only sin Jesus ever knew was mine," said A. W. Tozer, "and the only righteousness we'll ever know is His."[13]

In the kingdom of God, identity isn't achieved. Identity is received. It's part of a package deal that was purchased at Calvary's cross. In Christ, you are a new creation. You are the image of God. You are the apple of God's eye. You are God's workmanship. You are more than a conqueror. False humility is believing anything less, anything else. . . . Don't let anyone label you who didn't make you. If you do, those false labels turn into false narratives, false identities, and false idols. . . .

All our identity issues, in my opinion, are fundamental misunderstandings of who God is. Guilt issues are an underestimation of God's grace. Control issues are a misinterpretation of God's sovereignty. Pride issues are a miscalculation of God's greatness. Trust issues are a misapprehension of God's goodness.

—MARK BATTERSON, *A Million Little Miracles*

If God's identity is the foundation of your identity, then identity issues are a misunderstanding of who God is. How do you react to that statement?

_____

_____

Where do you see people struggling with identity in our culture?
How can finding our identity "in Christ" help with those issues?

_____

_____

_____

STUDY GOD'S WORD

God is good. We know that from Scripture. Yet from the beginning of human history, the Enemy has been undermining that truth. The father of lies, the accuser of the brethren, distracts us with the foolishness of fame and fortune, with power and prestige. His tactics haven't changed since Eden. Whenever he can, he tells us lies about who God is and who we are.

> The serpent was the shrewdest of all the wild animals the LORD God had made. One day he asked the woman, "Did God really say you must not eat the fruit from any of the trees in the garden?"
>
> "Of course we may eat fruit from the trees in the garden," the woman replied. "It's only the fruit from the tree in the middle of the garden that we are not allowed to eat. God said, 'You must not eat it or even touch it; if you do, you will die.'"
>
> "You won't die!" the serpent replied to the woman. "God knows that your eyes will be opened as soon as you eat it, and you will be like God, knowing both good and evil."

The woman was convinced. She saw that the tree was beautiful and its fruit looked delicious, and she wanted the wisdom it would give her. So she took some of the fruit and ate it. Then she gave some to her husband, who was with her, and he ate it, too. At that moment their eyes were opened, and they suddenly felt shame at their nakedness. So they sewed fig leaves together to cover themselves.

—GENESIS 3:1–7

Underline the lies Satan spoke to Eve in these verses. Where do you see the same lies represented and repeated in our world today?

_____

_____

_____

Take a moment to read 1 John 2:15–16. How do these verses relate to Satan's temptation of Adam and Eve? How do they connect with your experiences today?

_____

_____

_____

What was Satan's mission in the Garden of Eden? He wanted to make God seem less good than He really is. He used deception to imply that life in paradise was more difficult than it needed to be. *You're not allowed to eat from that tree? Really? Doesn't that sound restrictive?*

Satan plays to our negativity bias by shifting Adam and Eve's focus away from all the blessings they'd been given. Instead, he pointed their attention to perceived slights and apparent inconveniences. *God hasn't told you this stuff? Really? I wonder why He's keeping it a secret. . . .*

Before we move on, let's look at one more thing in Genesis 3:

> The LORD God said, "Look, the human beings have become like us, knowing both good and evil. What if they reach out, take fruit from the tree of life, and eat it? Then they will live forever!" So the LORD God banished them from the Garden of Eden, and he sent Adam out to cultivate the ground from which he had been made. After sending them out, the LORD God stationed mighty cherubim to the east of the Garden of Eden. And he placed a flaming sword that flashed back and forth to guard the way to the tree of life.
>
> —VERSES 22–24

We might be tempted to think God was being punitive by removing Adam and Eve from the garden. Why would He deny Adam and Eve access to the tree of life just because of one mistake? Why would He allow them to die?

The answer is that God didn't want humanity living forever in a sinful state. Can you imagine the sorrow of eternity in the presence of sin? Instead of making our sinfulness an eternal punishment, God removed our first ancestors from the garden and gave us the gift of death. Through Jesus, that gift allows us to experience eternity with Him in a dimension of reality that the Bible calls heaven.

How can we tell when we're focusing on inconveniences or problems rather than choosing to dwell on the blessings we've received? What are some characteristics of that way of living?

_____

_____

_____

How do you respond to the claim that death is a gift? Why is death a necessary element in God's plan for redemption?

_____

_____

_____

CARPE WONDER

Pages 157–59 of *A Million Little Miracles* introduce the idea of a life lie, which is a false belief that we build our lives around. It's the lie we tell ourselves to evade responsibility or to avoid hurt. A few examples? *I'm ugly. Therefore, I'm unlovable. Therefore, I will always be alone. Therefore, I may as well put up walls around my heart to protect myself from rejection.* Or how about this one? *My family was poor when I was a child, and we were miserable. Being wealthy would have solved all our problems and made us happy. Therefore, I will dedicate myself to getting wealthy now that I'm an adult so that I can be happy.*

These life lies are incredibly dangerous because they undermine our identity in Christ. They indict the person God created us to be while assaulting the goodness of God, in whose image we are designed.

The solution, of course, is to recenter and reaffirm our identity as children of God—the apple of His eye. You are beloved by God. You are God's workmanship regardless of what others may say. Don't let anyone label you who didn't make you!

MY MIRACLES: *Take a moment to identify any life lies that may have wormed their way into your heart and mind. What lies have you believed about yourself? If you have trouble recognizing the lies, start by thinking of things you don't like about yourself.*

_____

_____

_____

Throughout this week, pay attention to any moments in which those life lies rear their heads. Counter them by quoting Scripture to ground yourself in God's promises. What verses do you find helpful in countering your specific life lies?

_____

_____

_____

REMINDER: Read chapter 8 of *A Million Little Miracles* before engaging session 8 of this study guide.

CHASING BUTTERFLIES

Based on chapter 8 of *A Million Little Miracles.*

START WITH A MIRACLE

The largest seed in the world belongs to the Seychelles nut tree, also known as the double coconut. These seeds can weigh up to forty pounds![1] They also resemble a human posterior, which apparently can cause quite the stir for sailors when they see those seeds floating in the water off the coast of tropical islands.

When it comes to the smallest seed in the world, that honor belongs to the many varieties of orchids. Incredibly, orchid seeds can be as tiny as five-hundredths of a millimeter, which is smaller than a speck of dust! Orchid seeds don't include any food sources—no fruit material or nutmeat. Instead, the seeds must germinate inside or alongside another source of nutrition, such as various types of fungi.

Because of this, orchids reproduce by volume. Rather than drop dozens or hundreds or thousands of seeds like many trees and bushes, orchid seedpods each contain *millions* of seeds. Like spores, those seeds carpet-bomb the surrounding areas in the hope that a few will land in the middle of an environment necessary for germination of new life.

Take a moment to think about the latent potential of the orchid. One plant has the exponential ability to reproduce millions of other plants. Is that not miraculous? Seeds are the gift that keeps on giving.

That's how nature works—life gives rise to life. Of course, so does death. Whether you're a carnivore or herbivore, something *died* so you could live. Living things are inherently productive. They are designed to reproduce themselves. Think of all that a seed can become, if given half a chance. The power of a single seed is virtually incalculable.

On a scale of 1 (terrible) to 10 (wonderful), how would you rate yourself as a gardener? When have you been successful at helping something grow?

_____

_____

_____

What elements of your current situation are life-giving? Is there a person who is life-draining? A situation? What helps you be vital and productive?

_____

_____

_____

STUDY THE WORDS

This is a study about miracles, and one of the miracles we often overlook is the ongoing nature of creation. Like the present active imperative in the Greek language, it never stops. Creation is unfolding right in front of us, but it happens so slowly we can't see it. When we read the Genesis story, we tend to interpret those verses as describing something that happened past tense—

long, long ago, in a galaxy far, far away. That is true, but it's a half truth. God existed prior to the creation of our universe, which He initiated through His power and through His voice. That creation occurred long ago, but remember Hubble? The four words God spoke—"Let there be light" (Genesis 1:3)—are still creating galaxies at the edge of the universe.

Creation is still occurring, present tense. What God initiated at the moment of creation was not one and done. It's never-ending. Creation is still being created. And when we reach the end of human history as we know it, God will create a *new* heaven and a *new* earth.

When God created birds and fish and other animals, He didn't just create those early prototypes as one-offs. No, He created living things *that create living things*! And their ability to evolve is a testament to God's creativity. He gave life, which gives life.

> We read right over verses of Scripture that should cause us to audibly gasp in amazement. Just as hundreds of years of history are condensed in the genealogies, millions of species of plants are rooted in one verse. . . .
>
> > God said, "Let the land sprout with vegetation— every sort of seed-bearing plant, and trees that grow seed-bearing fruit."[2]
>
> Sounds simple enough, doesn't it? Not so fast. Just as four words—"Let there be light"—are still creating galaxies at the edge of the universe, these words—"Let the land sprout with vegetation"—are still bearing fruit. Of all God's inventions, the simple seed is one of the most miraculous.
>
> —MARK BATTERSON, *A Million Little Miracles*

What can we learn about God from the self-replicating nature of the universe He created?

_____

_____

_____

What are some specific ways we can join our Creator in bringing life into our world?

_____

_____

_____

One of the truths we've been trying to unravel throughout this study is that God is present and accounted for in nature. That may sound controversial because of the increasing prevalence of pantheism in our culture. If you're not familiar with that term, pantheism is the belief that nature *is* God. The natural world is how God is manifested in our universe. People who are true pantheists don't believe in a separate Being called God. Mother Nature is their god.

Obviously, that's not a biblical position. And that's not what I mean when I say God is present in nature. He's not just *in* nature; He's *over* the natural order. Simply put, creation is subject to its Creator. Even more, creation is powered and sustained by the Creator. In Him, we live and move and have our being.

We should be careful in how we make a distinction between sacred and secular. Too many people think that church is a place to learn about God and that nature is a place to learn about science. This is a false dichotomy. There's no domain devoid of God.

Every square inch of the universe belongs to the Creator. God owns the cattle on a thousand hills, and the hills! That means we can discover God, learn about God, and interact with God wherever we find ourselves.

> I've experienced some holy moments in church, at the altar.... I've experienced just as many holy moments at the beach, in the mountains, and under the stars. You can't raft the Colorado River through the Grand Canyon without worshipping. You can't hike the Inca Trail to Machu Picchu without praising. Most recently, we spent a few days with friends at Little Rocky Pond in Maine. Under the cover of night, we laid down on paddleboards and counted stars like Abram. It was a thin place. It was an open heaven. It was a two-foot field trip.
>
> —MARK BATTERSON, *A Million Little Miracles*

Where do you see our culture differentiating between sacred and secular? Where do you see that separation in the church?

_____

_____

_____

What does it look like to seek God both at church and in nature? What kinds of rhythms would be helpful for that approach?

_____

_____

_____

Part of what it means to worship God is praising Him for the blessings He has brought into our lives. That includes the material world. We should be grateful for sunsets and ocean waves and beautiful flowers and starry skies and the scent of vanilla and the sound of birds and the texture of grass and all the other wonders we encounter every day. We should thank God for those incredible blessings.

But another dimension of what it means to worship God is *enjoying* those blessings to the fullest. Should we feel guilty about how delicious Blue Bell ice cream tastes? Or Chick-fil-A chicken? Or the thirteen cuts of meat at Fogo de Chão? If bacon-wrapped steak is wrong, I don't want to be right!

Should we feel sheepish about spending time contemplating Scripture in the woods rather than in a sanctuary built by human hands? Should we be embarrassed about how awe-inspiring it is to witness the aurora borealis? Is there anything wrong with enjoying ocean waves, mountain views, or desert nights?

No, no, and no. We are making proper use of God's gifts when we enjoy those gifts. One way we steward them is by enjoying them—especially when we do so in a posture of gratitude. "Taste and see that the LORD is good" (Psalm 34:8).

God's greatest gifts are immaterial—spiritual rather than physical. It's the feeling of unconditional forgiveness or unmerited favor. It's joy unspeakable. It's a peace that passes understanding. It's the imagination that is part of the image of God. It's simple pleasures, not expensive toys. It's "raindrops on roses and whiskers on kittens."[3]

It's chasing butterflies, not catching them, that brings joy. It's wild and free. It's happy and holy. The journey is the destination, if you enjoy the journey. I can imagine Adam and Eve, butterfly nets in hand, romping around

Eden. What fun they must have had, and what joy that must have brought to the heart of a good God who delights in His playfellows.

—MARK BATTERSON, *A Million Little Miracles*

What does it look like to have a posture of gratitude toward God while we enjoy the blessings of this life?

_____

_____

_____

What is something you can do in the next few minutes to "taste and see that the LORD is good"?

_____

_____

_____

STUDY GOD'S WORD

Did you know there are two creation accounts in the book of Genesis? Not two different moments, of course, but two different versions of the same creation story, two different styles of telling that story. The first version in Genesis 1 offers a poetic and panoramic view of the beginning of everything. The camera is looking at God's creative actions through a wide-angle lens. The Hebrew word translated "God" in that chapter is *Elohim,* which implies "Creator."

In Genesis 2, the writer zoomed in for a much more intimate version of the creation story. The word translated "LORD" in that chapter is *Yahweh,* which is the name of the personal, covenantal God of Israel. Like color commentary, the second chapter focuses on God's relational involvement with Adam and Eve. He planted the garden. He formed Adam from the dust and Eve from a rib. He conversed with His creation.

> The LORD God planted a garden in Eden in the east, and there he placed the man he had made. The LORD God made all sorts of trees grow up from the ground—trees that were beautiful and that produced delicious fruit. In the middle of the garden he placed the tree of life and the tree of the knowledge of good and evil.
>
> A river flowed from the land of Eden, watering the garden and then dividing into four branches. The first branch, called the Pishon, flowed around the entire land of Havilah, where gold is found. The gold of that land is exceptionally pure; aromatic resin and onyx stone are also found there. The second branch, called the Gihon, flowed around the entire land of Cush. The third branch, called the Tigris, flowed east of the land of Asshur. The fourth branch is called the Euphrates.
>
> The LORD God placed the man in the Garden of Eden to tend and watch over it. But the LORD God warned him, "You may freely eat the fruit of every tree in the garden—except the tree of the knowledge of good and evil. If you eat its fruit, you are sure to die."
>
> —VERSES 8–17

Circle any words or phrases in the passage that show God's personal involvement with creation. To what degree is God personally involved with our world today?

How do these verses add to your understanding of God's nature and character?

Not only do we see God getting personally involved with His handiwork in Genesis 2, but we also see Him doing so in a way that feels hands-on. It's practical, even playful—especially when He lets Adam name the animals!

Perhaps these verses remind you of a child having fun with his or her toys:

The LORD God said, "It is not good for the man to be alone. I will make a helper who is just right for him." So the LORD God formed from the ground all the wild animals and all the birds of the sky. He brought them to the man to see what he would call them, and the man chose a name for each one. He gave names to all the livestock, all the birds of the sky, and all the wild animals. But still there was no helper just right for him.

So the LORD God caused the man to fall into a deep sleep. While the man slept, the LORD God took out one of the man's ribs and closed up the opening. Then the

LORD God made a woman from the rib, and he brought
her to the man.

—VERSES 18–22

*Where do you see evidence of God's playfulness in these verses? Where
do you see evidence that He was enjoying Himself throughout this
process?*

_____

_____

_____

*Why do we often assume that if something is fun, it can't be
spiritual? How might we have fun in a way that honors God and
blesses others?*

_____

_____

_____

CARPE WONDER

Did God have fun creating the universe? There is no way He
didn't. Then He also invited Adam to join in all the "reindeer
games"! More specifically, He offered Adam the chance to name
the animals found in and around the garden. Scripture says that
God "brought them to the man to see what he would call them."
You can feel the air of excitement, can't you?

There is a playfulness that is part and parcel of this creation
story. It's not unlike a child getting a new toy and then immediately wanting to show it to you—and give it a name. That's in-

nocence in action. That's pure delight. That's good old-fashioned fun!

Am I saying God was acting like a child? Kind of! "We have sinned and grown old," said G. K. Chesterton, "and our Father is younger than we."[4] The Ancient of Days somehow retains childlike characteristics, and He invites us to join Him in that carefree playtime. Will you do that this week? Will you join Him?

MY MIRACLES: *When was the last time you experienced something so fun that it made you feel like a kid again? How did you respond?*

_____

_____

_____

Where do you have an opportunity to invite others into a fun and playful experience this week? How can you connect that experience to worshipping and enjoying God?

_____

_____

_____

REMINDER: Read chapter 9 of *A Million Little Miracles* before engaging session 9 of this study guide.

LIFE IS BEAUTIFUL

Based on chapter 9 of *A Million Little Miracles*.

START WITH A MIRACLE

Where's the most beautiful place in the world? That's a tough question! There are so many places to choose from, and everybody's got their own opinion.

Some might say the Amalfi Coast of Italy, with its vineyards and mountains and picturesque villages built into the cliffs along the sea. Others might vote Japan during cherry blossom season. Then there's Taveuni—the Garden Island—in Fiji with its lush forests, its perfect beaches, and the largest variety of soft corals in the world. Or how about Zhangye National Geopark in China, which has a mountain range striated in the colors of the rainbow? It looks like it's straight out of Candy Land, but it's a veritable wonderland. Of course, there's also the Grand Canyon, Victoria Falls, the sandhills of the Sahara, and the grandeur of Nordic fjords.

There's no right answer. There's too much beauty in our world to settle on a single place as the hands-down winner.

Let me say that again: *There's too much beauty in our world!* We live on a planet with layers of loveliness and splendor and brilliance.

What a gift not only to live in this wonderland we call planet Earth but also to live in a time when we can travel almost anywhere by plane, train, or automobile. What a gift to witness so much wonder!

As we wrap up our study in this final session, we're going to praise God for the miracle of beauty—including the beauty of His mercies, which are new every morning. God makes all things beautiful in His time (Ecclesiastes 3:11). God even gives beauty for ashes (Isaiah 61:3).

Who sets the standards for beauty in our world today? How would you redefine those standards?

What are some of the ways you expose yourself to beauty? How might this move your heart to worship?

STUDY THE WORDS

Before original sin, there was the original lie. Sometimes we miss the full scope of that lie, focusing on the serpent's statement "You won't die!" Insert narrator's voice: "They did die!"

But look carefully at the full dialogue between the serpent and our earliest ancestors: "'You won't die!' the serpent replied to the woman. 'God knows that your eyes will be opened as soon as you eat it, and you will be like God, knowing both good and evil'" (Genesis 3:4–5). Satan promised Adam and Eve knowledge. He promised enlightenment—they would no longer be like little children running around the garden. They would instead elevate themselves to the same level as God. But that backfired.

In a twist of irony, what Satan said came true. Adam and Eve were no longer children after they ate the forbidden fruit. More specifically, they lost the gift of childlike innocence and, along with it, childlike wonder. In their attempt to become like God, they lost the pure delight of viewing the world through the eyes of a child.

There were thousands of fruit trees in that garden. Adam and Eve could eat almonds, apples, apricots, and avocados until the cows came home. There were fig trees, grapefruit trees, and peach trees. There was probably even a partridge in a pear tree!

My point? There were thousands of trees to enjoy— each one a miracle in its own right. Yet somehow the Enemy was successful in shifting their focus to the one and only tree that was off-limits. The Enemy's oldest trick is a tactic called forbidden fruit. Instead of enjoying a million little miracles, we get bent out of shape by one thing that isn't ours.

This is how the negativity bias enters the equation of human emotion. This is when and where and why we start playing the shame game, blame game, and fame game. Spoiler alert: The only way to win any of those games is to *not* play!

—MARK BATTERSON, *A Million Little Miracles*

What children do you interact with regularly? What words would you use to describe the way they approach the world?

Where do you see our culture pushing the lie that innocence and wonder are childish and unhelpful? How might seeing through that lie help you grow spiritually?

Many bad deals have been made in the history of the world. It's hard to believe that Russia sold Alaska to America for $7 million—roughly two cents per acre![1] But the worst deal in history, spiritually speaking, is what happened as a result of original sin. In that moment, we exchanged the miracle of innocence and wonder for the curse of sin and shame. The domino effect is still felt today.

Let's reverse engineer what happened: "Where are you?" God asked. Adam answered, "I heard you walking in the garden, so I hid. I was afraid because I was naked" (Genesis 3:9–10). And we've been hiding from God ever since! Traumatized by shame.

Have you noticed that young children have no shame about being naked? Kids love getting out of the bathtub and streaking around the house, glorying in their freedom to frolic. At some point, however, that freedom gets lost. Shame creeps in, and we make the same mistake that Adam and Eve did. We hide from ourselves, from others, and most significantly, from God.

> How do we overwrite those shame scripts? The same way we rewrite any negative narrative. Scripture is our script-cure! . . .
> Shame says, "I am a mistake."
> God says, "You are My workmanship."
> Shame says, "I am unworthy."
> God says, "You are worth the cross."
> Shame says, "I am not enough."
> God says, "You can do all things through Christ, who strengthens you."
> Shame says, "I am an accident."
> God says, "You are fearfully and wonderfully made."
> Shame says, "I am unlovable."
> God says, "You are My beloved."
> Shame says, "I am insignificant."
> God says, "You are the apple of My eye."
>
> —MARK BATTERSON, *A Million Little Miracles*

In what ways have you experienced the pain of guilt and shame? Can you recall a moment when you lost your innocence? How do you handle it?

What are the biggest obstacles that prevent you from believing that God loves you as much as He says He does throughout the Bible?

Wonder is a form of worship, so let me introduce an important word: *doxology*. You're already familiar with *theology*, which means "the study of God." Doxology is the worship of God. True theology always leads to doxology. Anything less is unhealthy and unholy. In the words of J. I. Packer, "The purpose of theology is doxology." The more we learn about God, the more opportunity we have to worship Him. Or to say it another way, learn more, worship more.

There are a million little miracles all around us. There are a million little miracles within us. We don't need lyrics on a screen to worship. We have plenty of other prompts! Each of those miracles is an opportunity to glorify God. When we don't take advantage of those opportunities, however, we begin to miss the miracles. And that's when we begin to miss God.

Ultimately, our lack of worship will cause us to drift toward idolatry, which is the worship of anything *but* God. The very real danger for us is that whatever we don't turn into praise turns into pride. Whatever we don't put on the altar turns into an idol. And as we learn from many Old Testament stories, this leads to a world of trouble.

> The imagination either builds altars or builds idols. If
> you worship self by setting up monuments, your world
> gets smaller and smaller and smaller. Eventually, the only
> thing that fits in your tiny little universe is *you*. If you
> worship God by building altars, your world gets bigger
> and bigger and bigger. True worship is the portal that

opens the door to a million little miracles! And you can worship Him in a million ways!

—MARK BATTERSON, *A Million Little Miracles*

Where do you see evidence of idolatry in the world today?

Where do you see evidence of idolatry in your own life? What can you do about it?

STUDY GOD'S WORD

Remember the conversation Jesus had with the woman at the well? It was a revelation for many reasons. That conversation ultimately unveiled His identity as the Messiah and led to her transformation. But before that, their conversation was about worship.

As you may remember, the Samaritans were an ethnic offshoot of Judaism. They were descendants of Jewish people who had intermarried with foreigners because of the different exiles during their nation's history. In fact, the Jews in Jerusalem hated the Samaritans and considered them to be spiritual half-breeds.

Jesus acknowledged some of those differences when He spoke with the woman about worship:

"Sir," the woman said, "you must be a prophet. So tell me, why is it that you Jews insist that Jerusalem is the only place of worship, while we Samaritans claim it is here at Mount Gerizim, where our ancestors worshiped?"

Jesus replied, "Believe me, dear woman, the time is coming when it will no longer matter whether you worship the Father on this mountain or in Jerusalem. You Samaritans know very little about the one you worship, while we Jews know all about him, for salvation comes through the Jews. But the time is coming—indeed it's here now—when true worshipers will worship the Father in spirit and in truth. The Father is looking for those who will worship him that way. For God is Spirit, so those who worship him must worship in spirit and in truth."

—JOHN 4:19–24

What does it mean to worship God in spirit? How should we understand that statement?

_____

_____

_____

What does it mean to worship God in truth? How would you describe the connection between truth and worship?

_____

_____

_____

As we've noted many times throughout these pages, everything that exists in our world is a gift from God. Everyday miracles are gifts from God that remind us of His presence, His power, His goodness, and His love.

Worship is simply offering these gifts back to Him. It's offering ourselves—time, talent, treasure—back to Him. It's a fundamental recognition that it's all *from* God and it's all *for* God.

Living life to the glory of God is "my utmost for His highest"—it means offering our very best to Him no matter what we are doing. When we sing, we sing with a heart filled with gratitude. When we work, we do our job so well that others take notice of our dedication—not for our own recognition but as a fragrant aroma pleasing to God. When we enjoy ourselves, we do so fully in the knowledge that our Father, the Source of all blessings, is worthy of every ounce of enjoyment we can muster.

Let the final psalm in the book of Psalms show you the way:

Praise the LORD!

Praise God in his sanctuary;
    praise him in his mighty heaven!
Praise him for his mighty works;
    praise his unequaled greatness!
Praise him with a blast of the ram's horn;
    praise him with the lyre and harp!
Praise him with the tambourine and dancing;
    praise him with strings and flutes!
Praise him with a clash of cymbals;
    praise him with loud clanging cymbals.
Let everything that breathes sing praises to the LORD!

Praise the LORD!

—PSALM 150

What principles can we glean from this psalm on what it means to worship?

What will you do this week to worship God in spirit and in truth? What will you do today?

CARPE WONDER

Did you know there are two types of praise? The first is glorifying God *after* we experience a blessing. I call this past-tense praise, and it's the most common form of worship because it makes the most sense. You say thanks after. We intuitively understand that kind of worship.

But there's another dimension of worship, a higher dimension of worship—future-tense praise. This is when we glorify God and thank Him *before* He does something on our behalf. I sometimes refer to this as *prophesying our praise* because that sentiment was expressed so often by the prophets. They would describe something God was about to do, and then they would glorify Him as if He had already done it.

God has promised to pour many blessings into our lives. Of course, there are conditions we must meet like obedience. But God has blessings in categories we can't even conceive of. There are many miracles we have yet to experience, but we have faith that we *will* experience them. Why? Because God said so. The old idiom is still true: God said it. I believe it. That settles it. We have many miracles to look forward to—not the least of which is our heavenly home, our glorified bodies, seeing God face-to-face, pain becoming past-tense, reuniting with our loved ones again, and so much more.

As we finish this study, take a moment to prophesy your praise for all the miracles God has already planned for your life! This is *not* "name it, claim it." It's simply standing on the promises of God. We worship a God who does not forget His people, does not forget His promise. This is the God who never over-promises or underdelivers. We worship the God of miracles—a million little miracles, and then some!

MY MIRACLES: *What are some prophetic words that have been spoken over your life? What are some of the promises God has made through His Word that you are banking on for the future?*

_____

_____

_____

Spend several minutes praising and thanking God that those promises will be delivered!

_____

_____

_____

Leader's Guide

Use the following pages to lead a group discussion and interaction for each of the sessions in this study. Remember to modify the number of questions based on the amount of time available for your gathering, and feel free to adapt the questions based on the needs of your group members.

SESSION 1: COUNT THE STARS

Start

When have you recently felt especially affected by the power or the beauty of nature? How did you respond?

Discuss

1. What did you enjoy most about session 1 of this study? Why?
2. Do you think technology is improving our lives or harming them? Explain.
3. Where would you draw the line between being comfortable and being too comfortable? How does this relate to your spiritual life?
4. Why are awe and wonder necessary ingredients in our lives?
5. What are some ways your life is stuck in ruts and routines? How might you inject some awe and wonder into your routines?

Study

Ask a volunteer to read Exodus 3:1–6 out loud; then discuss the following questions:

1. How does this passage connect with the theme of this session?
2. Moses needed to turn aside from his regular work in order to hear from God. What are some elements of our culture that can drag us away from what God wants us to experience?

Pray

Heavenly Father, we want to recognize Your presence in our lives each day. We want to acknowledge Your miracles! Please give us eyes to see the million little gifts You bring into our lives, and we will respond with praise.

In Jesus's name, amen.

SESSION 2: PLAYFELLOWS

Start

If you had to house a non-traditional pet (not a cat or dog) for a month, which type of animal would you choose? Why?

Discuss

1. When was the last time you remember feeling the emotion of wonder or amazement?
2. God has several attributes, including love, grace, wisdom, wrath, and justice. He also possesses the attribute of playfulness. Where do you see evidence of His playfulness reflected in our world?
3. What benefits do we receive as adults by indulging in playfulness and fun?

4. In your own words, how would you explain or summarize the concept of *tov*?
5. What are specific ways you have experienced God's goodness in the past month?

Study

Ask a volunteer to read Genesis 1:26–31 out loud; then discuss the following questions:

1. To what degree do human beings still possess the mission or assignment described in these verses?
2. Do you think our world is still "very good"? Explain.

Pray

Lord God, You are good, and You have created all things as a reflection of Your goodness. Please help us see that goodness as we work, play, and rest during this coming week. Please show us how to reflect Your goodness to everyone we meet.

In Jesus's name, amen.

SESSION 3: FLATLAND

Start

What does it look like for science and faith to work together?

Discuss

1. How would you define the concept of faith?
2. When have you recently had an opportunity to demonstrate faith in God? What happened?

3. In your opinion, do miracles still occur in our world? Why or why not?
4. When has God intervened in your life in a way that was especially meaningful? What happened next?
5. Where do you have an opportunity right now to take a leap of faith?

Study

Ask a volunteer to read Numbers 14:6–9 out loud; then discuss the following questions:

1. What do you like best about these verses? Why?
2. What steps can we take to overcome fear in our lives today?

Pray

Heavenly Father, we proclaim the truth that You are a God of miracles. You are sovereign over all things, including every detail of our lives. You are in control of every detail each day, and we are grateful to You. We praise Your name!
In Jesus's name, amen.

SESSION 4: HOLY CURIOSITY

Start

What are some words that describe your life's journey when it comes to physical health?

Discuss

1. In the personal study material, you wrote down a list of things you have to be grateful for. What were the most important items on that list?

2. How would you describe the relationship between gratitude and praising God?
3. What obstacles often prevent us from being grateful to God? What obstacles prevent us from offering praise to God?
4. In your own words, what is the difference between general revelation and special revelation? What are examples of each?
5. What are some of the ways you encounter God and interact with Him through His creation?

Study

Ask a volunteer to read Psalm 72 out loud; then discuss the following questions:

1. What are some of the main images present in this psalm? What do those images communicate?
2. Where do you see evidence of Solomon's holy curiosity in these verses?

Pray

Lord God, if we were to attempt to praise You for all that You have accomplished in our lives, we would have no time for anything else. You have given us so many good gifts! Please help us be more aware this week of opportunities to feel gratitude toward You, and please help us express that gratitude through verbal praise.

In Jesus's name, amen.

SESSION 5: SLEEPING BEAUTIES

Start

Vision is an example of an everyday miracle. When has the ability to see been an especially big blessing in your life?

Discuss

1. How does our culture view the interaction between science and faith?
2. In what ways do science and scientists help us recognize the million little miracles present in our world?
3. In what ways would your life be affected if you lost the ability to hear? What would you miss most?
4. How would you explain the difference between singing and worship? What transforms the former into the latter?
5. What are some elements of your everyday routine that hinder your ability to recognize the work and wonder of God in your life?

Study

Ask a volunteer to read Exodus 31:1–6 out loud; then discuss the following questions:

1. When has a work of art, a book, or a film caused you to feel awe or wonder? Why?
2. What do you appreciate most about worship with your church community? What do you appreciate most about worship on your own?

Pray

Heavenly Father, You have made it possible for us to enjoy the blessings of this world and to enjoy the incredible gift of fellowship with You. We say yes to every opportunity You place in front of us this week to experience joy, wonder, and worship. We say yes to You in every way!

In Jesus's name, amen.

SESSION 6: CONSIDER THE LILIES

Start

When has a person, an idea, or a new form of technology changed the way you see the world?

Discuss

1. To what degree are you able to focus on a specific object or task without getting distracted? Is that a strength or a weakness for you?
2. What is imagination? How would you define that concept?
3. Where do you see evidence of God's imagination and creativity in the world? In your own life?
4. The gift of physical touch and physical sensation plays a huge role in our lives. In what ways does your ability to touch something shape your ability to understand it?
5. What are the boundaries that should guide our use of touch when seeking to connect with others?

Study

Ask a volunteer to read Luke 8:43–48 out loud; then discuss the following questions:

1. How do these verses add to your understanding about Jesus's mission in our world?
2. What are some obstacles holding you back from reaching out to others—especially to those who are lonely or distressed?

Pray

Lord God, we affirm once again that You are the Creator of our minds and our bodies. You have blessed us with

imagination and the ability to reach out to one another with the gift of touch. You are the Source of our connection to You, to the world, and to one another. We say yes to those gifts!

In Jesus's name, amen.

SESSION 7: GOOD GOD

Start

When you hear the phrase *good person*, who comes to mind? Why?

Discuss

1. Part of the personal study for this session focused on the names of God. Which of those names caught your attention? Why?

2. The personal study also featured seven "I Am" statements that are connected with Jesus. How have you experienced Him in ways that align with those statements?

3. How would you define our culture's opinions about Jesus? What do people say about Him today?

4. What are some of the ways God's identity influences your identity? (How are they connected?)

5. When have you been able to experience God's goodness in an especially meaningful way? How might we increase our daily awareness of His goodness?

Study

Ask a volunteer to read Genesis 3:1–7 out loud; then discuss the following questions:

1. What are some specific ways Satan attempted to chip away at Adam and Eve's understanding of God's goodness?
2. What are some ways we can proclaim or reflect God's goodness in our community today?

Pray

Heavenly Father, we declare once again that You are good in every way. There is nothing about You that is not wonderful, beautiful, and worthy of praise. Because that is true, we are deeply grateful that You have created us in Your image. Please work this week to reveal the goodness and loveliness inside us all.

In Jesus's name, amen.

SESSION 8: CHASING BUTTERFLIES

Start

What parts of your regular routine are life-giving? What about your day fills you up rather than draining you dry?

Discuss

1. What did you find surprising from this session? Why?
2. God is the original Creator of all things, but that creation is still ongoing; life is still producing life. What is our role in the process of creation today?
3. How would you describe the difference between pantheism and the biblical view of God's connection with the created world?
4. Our culture actively pushes a separation between what is sacred and what is secular. Do you think this is a good idea? Why or why not?

5. Because God created the gift of nature, we worship God by enjoying that gift. How can we enjoy the blessings of creation in ways that honor the Creator?

Study

Ask a volunteer to read Genesis 2:8–17 out loud; then discuss the following questions:

1. What are some of the ways God encouraged Adam and Eve to enjoy His creative work?
2. Many people think that if something is fun, it can't be spiritual. How would you respond to that concept?

Pray

Lord God, we recognize that You are the Creator of all things. Not only that, but You are also the Sustainer of all things. If You were to remove Yourself from creation even for a moment, all that we know would collapse. Therefore, we praise You, Lord God. We praise Your power and Your creativity and Your playfulness.

In Jesus's name, amen.

SESSION 9: LIFE IS BEAUTIFUL

Start

People have different opinions about the most beautiful place in the world. What's your opinion?

Discuss

1. What have you appreciated most from this study, or what have you enjoyed most? Why?

2. In their desire to gain knowledge, Adam and Eve lost their innocence. Where do you see that same loss of innocence happening today?

3. In what ways have you seen the destructive consequences of guilt and shame in our modern world?

4. What are some of the obstacles that hinder us from believing that God loves us? That He likes us?

5. Given everything we've learned about God's role in our world and everyday miracles, why is idolatry such a harmful practice?

Study

Ask a volunteer to read Psalm 150 out loud; then discuss the following questions:

1. Why is worship a necessary part of our existence? Of our everyday lives?

2. What does it look like for you to worship God in spirit and in truth?

Pray

Heavenly Father, we are so grateful for everything You have taught us during this study. We are grateful for everything You have helped us experience and enjoy. We ask that Your Holy Spirit cement these lessons and principles in our hearts and minds as we make our way in this world each day. Thank You, God, for Your greatness, goodness, and love!

In Jesus's name, amen.

NOTES

A Note from Mark

1. Elizabeth Howell and Doris Elin Urrutia, "How Fast Is Earth Moving?," Space.com, updated October 19, 2023, www.space.com/33527-how-fast-is-earth-moving.html.

Session 1: Count the Stars

1. Robert Michael Pyle, quoted in Masashi Soga and Kevin J. Gaston, "Extinction of Experience: The Loss of Human-Nature Interactions," *Frontiers in Ecology and the Environment* 14, no. 2 (2016): 94, https://extension.unh.edu/sites/default/files/migrated_unmanaged _files/Resource007361_Rep10598.pdf.
2. Psalm 46:10.
3. Hope Reese, "How a Bit of Awe Can Improve Your Health," *New York Times,* January 23, 2023, www.nytimes.com/2023/01/03/well/ live/awe-wonder-dacher-keltner.html.
4. Michael Dregni, "How Exercise Benefits the Brain," Experience Life, April 26, 2018, https://experiencelife.lifetime.life/article/this-is-your-brain-on-exercise.
5. Mark Batterson, *Draw the Circle: The 40 Day Prayer Challenge* (Grand Rapids, Mich.: Zondervan, 2012).

Session 2: Playfellows

1. C. S. Lewis, *God in the Dock: Essays on Theology and Ethics,* ed. Walter Hooper (Grand Rapids, Mich.: William B. Eerdmans), 13.
2. "What Is Lightning?," National Weather Service: NWS Flagstaff, AZ, accessed June 24, 2024, www.weather.gov/fgz/Lightning.

3. Matthew 18:3.

4. Theodor Geisel, "Dr. Seuss Quotes," BrainyQuote, accessed May 3, 2024, www.brainyquote.com/quotes/dr_seuss_106059.

5. "Shorter Catechism," Orthodox Presbyterian Church, accessed May 20, 2024, https://opc.org/sc.html.

Session 3: Flatland

1. Govert Schilling, "Does the Universe Expand Faster Than Light?," *BBC Sky at Night,* January 26, 2024, www.skyatnightmagazine.com/space-science/does-universe-expand-faster-than-light.

2. Thomas Aquinas, *Summa Contra Gentiles,* book 1, *God,* trans. and ed. Anton C. Pegis (Notre Dame, Ind.: University of Notre Dame Press, 2014), chap. 13.

3. John 11:43, KJV.

4. Romans 8:31.

5. Romans 8:11.

6. Philippians 4:13.

7. A. W. Tozer, *The Knowledge of the Holy: The Attributes of God; Their Meaning in the Christian Life* (New York: Harper & Row, 1961), 6.

8. Tozer, *Knowledge,* 10.

Session 4: Holy Curiosity

1. D. Lozano-Ojalvo, R. López-Fandiño, and I. López-Expósito, "PBMC-Derived T Cells," in *The Impact of Food Bioactives on Health: In Vitro and Ex Vivo Models,* ed. Kitty Verhoeckx et al. (New York: Springer, 2015), https://doi.org/10.1007/978-3-319-16104-4_16.

2. Leviticus 17:11.

3. James Gallagher, "More Than Half Your Body Is Not Human," BBC, April 9, 2018, www.bbc.com/news/health-43674270.

4. Cindy Stellar, "Gratitude and Anxiety Cannot Coexist," Noomii, May 24, 2023, www.noomii.com/articles/13710-gratitude-and-anxiety-cannot-coexist.

5. Hayim Nahman Bialik and Yehoshua Hana Ravnitzky, eds., *The Book of Legends: Legends from the Talmud and Midrash*, trans. William G. Braude (New York: Schocken Books, 1992), 533:250.

6. C. S. Lewis, *Surprised by Joy: The Shape of My Early Life* (San Francisco: HarperOne, 2017), 6, 19.

Session 5: Sleeping Beauties

1. "CRISPR Therapy Restores Some Vision to People with Blindness," *Nature*, May 9, 2024, www.nature.com/articles/d41586-024-01285-0.

2. Fred Hoyle, quoted in Ron Carlson and Ed Decker, *Fast Facts on False Teachings* (Eugene, Ore.: Harvest House, 1994), 57.

3. Psalm 19:1, NIV.

4. Monica C. Parker, *The Power of Wonder: The Extraordinary Emotion That Will Change the Way You Live, Learn, and Lead* (New York: TarcherPerigee, 2023), 9.

Session 6: Consider the Lilies

1. Christoph Irmscher, *Louis Agassiz: Creator of American Science* (New York: Houghton Mifflin Harcourt, 2013), 3.

2. Lulu Miller, *Why Fish Don't Exist: A Story of Loss, Love, and the Hidden Order of Life* (New York: Simon and Schuster, 2020), 71.

3. Louis Agassiz, quoted in Irmscher, *Louis Agassiz*, 150.

4. Hebrews 10:25.

5. "Media Tip Sheet: Chamber of Commerce Data: Washington D.C. Is the 'Loneliest City' in America," GW Media Relations, February 2024, https://mediarelations.gwu.edu/media-tip-sheet-chamber-commerce-data-washington-dc-loneliest-city-america.

Session 7: Good God

1. Joseph Goldstein, "$1 Billion Donation Will Provide Free Tuition at a Bronx Medical School," *New York Times*, February 26, 2024, www.nytimes.com/2024/02/26/nyregion/albert-einstein-college-medicine-bronx-donation.html.

2. Exodus 15:26.

3. Genesis 22:14.

4. Numbers 6:24, 27, NIV.

5. 2 Corinthians 5:21.

6. "967 Names and Titles of God," ChristianAnswers.net, https:// christiananswers.net/dictionary/namesofgod.html.

7. John 1:14.

8. John 6:35; 8:12; 10:7, 11; 11:25; 14:6; 15:5.

9. Eugene Peterson, *Tell It Slant: A Conversation on the Language of Jesus in His Stories and Prayers* (Grand Rapids, Mich.: Eerdmans, 2008), 211.

10. Colossians 1:15, NIV.

11. John 1:14.

12. See, for example, Romans 8:16; 2 Corinthians 6:18; 1 John 3:1.

13. A. W. Tozer, *Toward a More Perfect Faith: 4 Stages in Your Pursuit of God* (Chicago: Moody, 2023).

Session 8: Chasing Butterflies

1. Larry Hodgson, "The Double Coconut: The World's Largest Seed," The Laidback Gardener, November 25, 2018, https://laidback gardener.blog/2018/11/25/the-double-coconut-the-worlds-largest-seed.

2. Genesis 1:11.

3. "My Favorite Things," by Richard Rodgers and Oscar Hammerstein II, *The Sound of Music*, directed by Robert Wise (Robert Wise Productions and Argyle Enterprises, 1965).

4. G. K. Chesterton, *Orthodoxy* (CreateSpace, 2018), 30.

Session 9: Life Is Beautiful

1. "Check for the Purchase of Alaska (1868)," National Archives, www.archives.gov/milestone-documents/check-for-the-purchase-of-alaska.

Also from bestselling author
MARK BATTERSON

Be reminded of the millions of miracles God performs every day, and be inspired to live with a clearer sense of identity and purpose.

Dig into the Bible with this compelling companion study guide. Engage with key questions and activities, and note the ways God reveals His greatness and reminds us of His goodness.

 MULTNOMAH

Learn more about Mark Batterson's books at
waterbrookmultnomah.com.